14 Days

14 Days

a mother, a daughter, a two-week goodbye

Lisa Goich

· A SAVIO REPUBLIC BOOK ·

A SAVIO REPUBLIC BOOK
ISBN: 978-1-61868-560-5
ISBN (eBook): 978-1-61868-559-9

14 DAYS
A Mother, A Daughter, A Two-Week Goodbye
© 2015 by Lisa Goich
All Rights Reserved

Cover Design by Ryan Truso
Interior design and typesetting by Neuwirth & Associates

For my Mother.
The wind beneath my wings.

Preface

"I want Mitch Albom to write me a eulogy," my mom said in an expectant tone.

"Mother, everyone wants Mitch to write their eulogy."

"Yes, but he likes me. Ask him to write one for me."

"Mother, I can't . . . I . . ."

She looked at me with dying eyes, mother eyes. Eyes saying, "just do it."

"But, I don't want to ask him for a favor like this. It makes me uncomfortable."

"Lisa, just ask him. All he can do is say no."

Foreword

Millie –

Although these are difficult last days, I have no doubt where you are going next. You'll be in heaven with a first class ticket.

In case you are overwhelmed by the beauty when you arrive and you find yourself temporarily speechless, here is a piece of paper that you can present to whoever is manning the gates, OK?

It can serve as your official introduction.

We loved you every minute you were with us – and will for all the minutes to come.

God bless you on your journey home.

Love,
Mitch Albom

Hello, my name is Millie Goich, or, if your records go way back, Mila Birach, born March 5, 1926. You shouldn't need to look me up. My friends tell me my reputation precedes me.

I'm happy to be here. I was ready to be here. I have been dreaming of this place for a while. I'm eighty-five years old, and people tell me I filled those eighty-five years with as much love and laughs as one person can expect from a life on earth. Now it's time to check out the new digs. If you have any space that looks like Las Vegas, you can sign me up. And if you have any Wizard of Oz slot machines, that would be fine, too. I mean, if you can't get lucky here, where can you?

As for me? Well. I know this: I had a great life. If you measure your success by those you leave behind and how fondly they think of you, I hit the jackpot.

I count three children, two grandchildren, one great grandchild, and an adoring, loving husband from my time on earth, which is a good life's work no matter who you're talking about. My kids tell me I always put them first and never thought about myself. They're being sweet. But my family really did come first. I didn't mind. That's how I wanted to live.

In fact, if you've got some families up here you want me to watch after—cook, fuss, whatever you need—I can make the time. Making time comes easily for me. I've done it all my life.

I think it comes from being loved. My husband and I fell for each other the day we met, at a weenie roast. Sixty-four great years together. Do you know, after all that time, we still hold hands? I can feel his hand in mine even now. Sometimes you just know. I was blessed that way.

I also got to make a lot of fond and funny memories. I teased people. I gave them a little sass. I loved to laugh. I even worked at a donut shop for a while, and traded some back and forth jokes with the cops. Do you know what cops are? I don't suppose you need any up here.

My kids tell me I was devoted and dedicated and that I never stopped worrying. Well, they're right about the last part. You always worry about your children. But I'm hoping now that I'm here, I'll see there is actually nothing to worry about. It would be nice to get that message to the kids. Then again, we can let them sweat it out, if it keeps them in line. It'll be our little secret.

I do have a couple of questions. Do you keep up with the Kardashians up here, too? If so, I'm prepared. If not, that's okay, too. However, if you separate the neighborhoods here by political parties, I would like to sleep with the Democrats. Force of habit. Sorry.

Mostly, you can count on me for cooking, joking, Yugoslavian detail work, moral support and endless love. I am kind of like that song, "Bridge Over Troubled Water."

I love that tune. And that's what my family and loved ones say about me. If they're right, who am I to argue? All I can tell you is I had a great life, I lived it on my terms as much as I could, and based on all the smiles—and tears—at the end, I must have done something right.

I'm just happy to be here. I didn't want to get on the bus going south, if you know what I mean.

If God is reading this, thank you for all you gave me on earth—and for the chance I had to give some of it back. I really do see what you mean when you say to give is to live. That's how I handled it. And I feel more alive than ever.

So . . . let's get this second act started, right?

Sincerely yours,

Millie Goich

Beloved wife, mother, mother-in-law, grandmother, relative and cherished friend of too many people to count

This is a special little book about love, and a mother and a daughter and saying goodbye. You might see yourself in this book, or you might just be here to experience the story. Regardless, I welcome you to take my hand and step inside my parents' house and share in my mother's final days with me. Thank you for coming. Make sure you take some cookies home with you when you leave.

14 Days

Day 1

DECEMBER 11

"Dashing through the snow, in a one horse open sleigh . . ."

I thought burning my toast was going to be the worst thing that happened today. It wasn't just the fact that the toast was burnt, it was the last two pieces of bread in the package. I had no backup plan. While my dad sat at the kitchen table eating his oatmeal, and my dog Angie sat on the floor at his side waiting for table scraps, I tossed the bread in the garbage and cursed my brother under my breath for distracting me with his phone call. My first full day back in my hometown of Warren, Michigan wasn't starting on a high note. My parents' toaster was half to blame. Because the toaster didn't turn off on its own, toasting required staring at the bread through the red-hot slots and, when it looked like it was browned, manually pushing the button to pop it out. My mom and dad never felt the need to get a new toaster. When you're eighty-five and eighty-nine respectively, I guess watching things cook isn't that big of a deal. What else have you got to do? They could see their TV from the kitchen, so while the bread was browning they'd have one finger on the button and one eye on *Good Morning America* in the other room.

Perhaps if my brother Richard didn't call with an urgent message to get to the hospital "Now!" I wouldn't have started this Sunday with a grumbling stomach and a bug up my butt. My mom had been admitted to the hospital two days prior after a fall at the kidney dialysis center left her unable to walk. I had gone straight from the airport to the hospital the evening before after arriving in Detroit from Los Angeles. My dad and I planned on a leisurely morning at home before joining my mom again at her bedside. Obviously leisurely wasn't in the plans today and there was some news my brother chose not to share with my dad and me over the phone, but insisted we hear in person. That's never good. It seems to be status quo in my family. No one tells anyone anything for fear of upsetting them. People in our family have gone in and out of hospitals, have had strokes, heart attacks and cancer, have gone through chemo and remission, all before other family members were told about it. "She doesn't need to worry," they'd say in hushed tones, putting their index finger to their lips. My mom had a tumor and eighteen inches of her colon removed five years earlier and was home healing before my niece even knew she was sick. She's sensitive, they say. So they keep the bad stuff from her, hoping she'll never find out.

But today, while my brother's urgent "Now!" lingered in the air, I would soon be in on the secret.

"Are you ready?" asked my dad, already standing at the back door with his keys in hand.

"Am I ready? Do I look ready?" I asked, motioning down the length of my body to my pajamas and bare feet. "Give me five minutes," I added, and went back into my bedroom.

I heard my dad let out a big *huff* as he jingled his keys in his gloved hands, obviously frustrated that he couldn't leave right away.

My parents always had a way of guilting me into not being late. They were never late. Ever. My mom packed for vacations a week before she was leaving. The airport? She'd leave seven hours ahead of takeoff, "just in case."

So today, as my dad stood in the doorway with his coat on muttering under his breath, I hurriedly threw on the same clothes I wore on the plane the day before, tossed my little dog, Angie, into her carrier bag, pulled a baseball cap over my frizzy curls and headed back into the family room.

"Okayyyyy . . . let's go," I said, rolling my eyes, feeling more like a fifteen-year-old than a woman on the brink of fifty.

As my dad pressed the button to the left on the wall, next to his *Parking For Serbians Only!* sign, the electric door lifted and the morning sun poured into the garage, followed by a biting gust of wind and a swirl of snow. It had started snowing about an hour earlier and a blanket of white had accumulated on the driveway. The wind whipped the trees and tossed the snowflakes, reminding me why I left this northern climate sixteen years ago. Living in Los Angeles for more than a decade, I rarely ventured home to Michigan in the winter. I don't ski, I'm not a fan of winter sports and I have spent far too many hours on airplanes warding off panic attacks waiting for planes to de-ice before taking off. Detroit was far more appealing to me in May than it was in December.

I buckled Angie's carrier into the back seat then climbed into the passenger side of my dad's Jeep Liberty SUV. This was my mom's side of the car and it seemed odd that I was sitting there and not in the back seat with my dog. Dad in the driver's seat. Mom in the passenger seat. Kids in the back seat. Isn't that the way it always was and always should be? I stared at my mom's used tissue wadded up in the cup holder and got a foreboding sadness as my dad turned the key to the Jeep's ignition. My dad—a loyal Chrysler employee even twenty-five years post-retirement—only drove

Chrysler products. We rarely mention my Toyota Prius around him. It inevitably brings up lectures of "The Japs" and World War II and buying American and recessions and depressions. I'd rather talk about the fuel efficiency, but he'll have nothing of it.

As my dad backed down the driveway, the Liberty dovetailed a bit as he shifted from reverse to drive when he reached the street. We headed toward the freeway, the main streets slick from the new-fallen snow. I forgot how nerve-wracking it was to be in a car with my dad. At eighty-nine, he drove like a sixteen-year-old boy. Revving up to speeds about twenty miles over the speed limit, he has always had a habit of racing to the car in front of him, then slamming on his brakes just as he was about to make contact with the car's rear bumper. This day was no different. Each time he'd speed and stop, my feet inevitably found their way to the dashboard, pushing down hard as the red lights in front of us grew closer. My hand clutched the handle above the passenger door and I could feel my fingernails burrowing into my palm, anticipating the moment of impact that we miraculously missed every time. I knew better than to say anything. My dad wasn't a fan of backseat drivers and never took to criticism of his automotive handling skills very well. Perhaps that's a cockiness one develops after building cars for thirty-plus years.

Trying to keep my mind off the driving—and the "Now!" that awaited us at the hospital—I attempted to strike up a conversation with my dad that would bring both of our minds to a different place. Talking to my dad one-on-one was always a very stilted venture. Most of our conversations during my life took place with my mom as a go-between. A sort of translator between the two of us. When I would call home, and my dad answered the phone, before I could even get out a "hello," he'd say, "Here's your mother," and hand her the phone. We never had much to talk about, I guess. And that morning wasn't any different.

"Soooooo . . ." I said, drawing out the word 'so,' hoping that it would trigger a topic, or at least six or eight more words to complete a full sentence. "I see they remodeled the Taco Bell," pointing to the fast-food restaurant our family frequented often.

My dad, just as awkward in his response said, "Yeah, it's been a couple years now. Your mother likes Taco Bell. She likes those chalupas. That's some good Mexican food, that Taco Bell."

"Those chalupas are good," I added, wishing we could actually pull through the drive-thru and order a couple.

Before moving to California, Taco Bell was the only Mexican food I had ever eaten. Warren, Michigan—a suburb of Detroit—isn't known for its ethnic diversity. Nor its culinary dining experiences. With restaurants with names like "J. Edgar's On Hoover," it was a buffalo wings and meat and potatoes kind of town. Blue-collar cuisine. Dinner rolls presented in plastic baggies. Three-dollar breakfast specials.

As we continued toward the freeway, we passed my high school. It, too, had received a facelift since last I visited. But the giant dome we once climbed on our senior year and spray painted was still intact. I couldn't even fathom climbing on top of a building now, let alone destructing property or spray painting without a mask. Even though I knew it was wrong to do back then, the sixteen-year-old me never thought about consequences. Or heights. Or toxic chemical fumes.

Thankfully the freeway had been salted, as my dad sped down the ramp onto Interstate 696. With my mind completely void of any further conversation, I reached down and turned on the radio. Faith Hill's "Come Home" poured from the speakers, foreshadowing the afternoon's topic of conversation.

After a thirty-five-minute drive, we arrived at Grosse Pointe's Beaumont Hospital. Grosse Pointe, Michigan is located on the shore of Lake St. Clair, bordering the city of Detroit. The two cities are a stark contrast: Detroit, urban and gritty; Grosse Pointe, sparkling in its storied glory. The Grosse Pointes, as they are collectively referred to (they're so fancy, there isn't just one, but five communities in all: Grosse Pointe,

Grosse Pointe Park, Grosse Pointe Shores, Grosse Pointe Woods and Grosse Pointe Farms), are known for their money and quaint small-town feel. Lakeshore Drive is home to some of the stateliest mansions in the country. Big money. Old money. Dodge and Ford kind of money. I always envisioned myself marrying a doctor or the son of some sort of shipping magnate or furniture store chain owner and living along Lakeshore Drive. I'd have a boat, three children and a lot of brightly colored Lilly Pulitzer clothes in my closet. Instead I moved to California, married a rock musician, found solace in a 1,100 square foot house in the stifling hot San Fernando Valley and never saw my uterus reach its full rental potential. And black became my clothing color of choice. I've never ruled out that boat, however.

As my dad slid into a parking space at the hospital, I wiped the sweat from my palms onto the pant legs of my jeans and climbed out of the Jeep, thankful we arrived unscathed. I slipped Angie's bag over my shoulder and pulled my scarf over my face as we walked toward the hospital's entrance. "Fuck, it's freezing here," I said to myself as the wind seemed to instantly harden the tears in my eyeballs. "Fuck" was the only word one could use to describe Great Lakes winter cold. "Heck" just didn't cut it. "Yikes" was an understatement. Why did I always forget how numbingly frigid Michigan winters were? It must be some sort of survival mechanism—the same one that makes you forget how crappy an ex-boyfriend was after you've broken up. All your brain can remember are the happy times and sunshine.

The sliding automatic doors opened to a whoosh of warm air as we stomped our wet boots on the floor mat and made our way to the front desk. "Millie Goich," we informed the receptionist, as she gave us our guest badges to gain admission to my mother's floor. Shielding Angie's bag with my elbow so the security guard wouldn't see I was bringing a dog into the hospital, the three of us headed upstairs to room 216.

Like a tiny rag doll sitting in a giant hospital bed, my mother looked like she had aged twenty years overnight. Her seventy-pound body was swimming in her nightgown. A giant black and purple bruise, caused by the port for her kidney dialysis, covered her chest. Her once thick head of pepper and salt hair (still more pepper than salt) seemed sparse, the curls gathered to one side revealing an oversized ear on the other. A shoulder bone poked through the upper arm of her nightgown. Her collarbone was so pronounced, it looked as if you could rest a book on it. She was so fragile, I hesitated to even lean on her when I bent over to kiss her cheek. I settled at the foot of the bed holding a shivering Angie in my arms, and my dad sat at my mom's right side holding her hand. My brother, fourteen years my senior, who had been at the hospital since earlier that morning, was sitting in a chair across from us. "How'd you sleep, Mother?" I asked, as cheerily as I could, while fixating on the solid blue circles under her vacant eyes. "Have you tried to walk yet?"

Most of my adult life, I called my mom by the formal name of Mother. I'd refer to her as, "my mom," but always called her Mother. Both my brother and sister called her Mother as well. And my dad, Father. I don't know how that started, or why. We weren't a fancy family. We were from Detroit, for goodness sake, not a wealthy, aristocratic suburb. But it's what we called them and it stuck. It was uncomfortable to refer to my parents in any other way.

Ignoring the questions in front of her, my mom—never one to mince words—replied in her Edith-Bunker-meets-Fran-Drescher-voice, "I'm done with dialysis." Not "Hello." "How are you?" "How was your morning?" But, "I'm done with dialysis."

My eyes darted to my brother for clarification, then back to my mom. "You don't need dialysis anymore?" optimistically misunderstanding the underlying meaning of her statement.

"I'm done with dialysis. I don't want it anymore." She waved her hand dismissively in the air and said, "Just let me go. I want to go."

My head started processing the information like the inside of a computer. Stringing together ones and zeroes. Processing. Processing. Trying to grasp what that meant.

'Go. Just let me go.' She was saying she wanted to die.

My. Mom. Was. Going. To. Die.

I got it. I totally understood. She was saying she could no longer live with the fatigue and nausea and discomfort that the three-day-a-week treatments burdened her with. Who could blame her? One good day, one bad day, another good day, another bad day, a third good day, another bad day. At eighty-five, she was finally ready to call her own shots. Who was I to argue? Though I understood it, it would be days before I could actually wrap my mind around the truth of it all.

I often wondered how this particular movie would end. Would I receive a late-night call from my brother saying my mom had passed away? Would my dad call in tears saying my mom didn't wake up one morning? For years, every time the phone rang in the middle of the night, my heart would race, fearing someone on the other end would tell me my mom was gone. The end had finally been written. And I was strangely okay with it. For now.

I wondered if this is how my mom thought she was going to make her exit. Did seventeen-year-old pixie spitfire Mildred Birach—voted

Best Dressed her senior year at Southeastern High School in Detroit, with her perfectly manicured nails and platformed, open-toed shoes—ever imagine that, nearly seventy years later, she would lie in a tattered nightgown in a hospital bed calling her own death sentence? Do any of us ever think about that day? We're rarely privy to our final fate. And it's probably best that way. Millie Goich most likely wouldn't have imagined it would have been her kidneys that ended it all. Cancer maybe. Some complication from all those years of smoking, perhaps. But kidneys? Probably not.

But what she did know was that she was ready to roll. My mom was going to die. We weren't sure when it would happen, but knew it would be at some point in the near future. It was something I couldn't quite comprehend when it was plopped right there on my lap in front of me. The person who let go of my hand when I took my first steps, the person who released the back of my bicycle seat when I pedaled on two wheels for the first time, the person who grounded me when I got drunk on Mad Dog 20/20 in high school, the person who sat on the kitchen floor with me when I sobbed my eyes out over a boy, the person who told me I was the most precious gift she ever received and that she was so glad I was born—that person told me she was done. Fin. Over. The end.

At the announcement, I surprisingly didn't even shed a tear. I just looked at her and nodded my head in agreement. It certainly wasn't the response I would have thought I'd have had when my mom told me she was going to die. Years earlier when I first moved to California and started acting lessons, one of the things I learned was how to cry on command. We were taught to think about a sad moment in our past, or the possible death of a loved one, in order to muster up tears. I always used the fictitious death of my mother to elicit a watershed. But today, when it was actually laid out before me, not a tear was in sight. And I tried. Believe me, I tried. But somehow I think I absorbed my mom's peace of mind and, instead of weeping for the loss I'd be facing, I embraced the sense of calm that my mom finally had found. I looked into her eyes—a shade of grey-blue clouded by cataracts—and said, "I support your decision." She shook her head in acknowledgement and, emotionless, without saying a word, looked up at the TV as Vanna White revealed three Rs in the puzzle that was a "Thing."

And with that, I fished through my purse for my phone, texted my boss and said, "I'm not going to be in for a while."

And so began Day 1 of what would become a fourteen-day vigil. Millie Goich—The Farewell Tour.

❇

I felt such a strong moment of serenity in the hours following my mom's announcement. I think the feeling was emanating off her. She was so sure of her decision, it was hard to look at her and not go along with the plan. She was tired. She was frail. At less than seventy pounds, unable to walk, little bowel control, extreme back pain from years of severe osteoporosis and scoliosis—it was no wonder she was ready to close the door. I fully understood. And when she finally said it out loud, I could see the tranquility come over her. Like an aura, it enveloped her. Purple light. Healing light. For the first time in years, I sensed that my mother was truly happy. When we give up control, we find peace. And Millie Goich was finally at peace.

Unfortunately, the support I felt for my mom's decision wasn't universal among the other members of our immediate family. I could empathize with their stance. No one wanted to see my mom die. But I also understood that if she lived another day, it would be worse to her than death could ever be. My brother already knew of my mom's decision as she revealed it to my dad and me. That's why he insisted we rush to the hospital. That's why I burnt my toast. He stood at the foot of the bed and watched as I shook my head in agreement when my mom told us she wanted to stop her dialysis. I knew by his glare and the way he bit his lip—a nervous habit he's had his whole life—that we weren't on the same team. He expected me to challenge her. To ask her to rethink her decision. But I didn't.

There were arguments in the hospital that day and a lot of tears. Siblings tugging at the "she should live, no, she should die" rope. An argument between my brother and me in the hallway escalated to the point that nurses were shushing us. Patients shuffled by with IVs attached to their arms—their behinds hanging out the backs of their hospital gowns—looking at us nervously as arms were flailing and words were flying. Family members of other patients were poking their heads out of rooms, trying to see what the commotion was at the end of the hall. I just wanted to crawl into my mom's bed with her, get under the covers and never come out.

"This isn't your decision to make, Richard. It's *hers*. Hers and hers alone. Now *stop*."

A gentleman quickly withdrew his head from the hallway door when he saw me look in his direction.

My brother's face was bright red as he continued to question me for supporting my mom in her decision to die. What I wasn't seeing in my brother's eyes was that he was scared. Not angry. He was hurt so deeply at the thought of losing my mom that he lashed out the only way he knew best.

Being a religious man, Richard was fearful of my mom's fate, should she decide to take her life—and in this case, death—into her own hands.

"This is *suicide*, you know that, right?" exclaimed my brother through tears. "Suicide! In our church, this is suicide. She won't go to heaven if she kills herself. And stopping dialysis is killing herself."

In a rational state of mind I would know this was a common concern. Surely other people had had these same thoughts when their loved ones decided to stop chemo or go into hospice. He wasn't alone in his consternation. But at that moment, neither of us could see beyond our own argument. And—each inheriting my mom's stubborn gene—were in it to win it.

Heaven. Hell. Life. Death. I couldn't even process what was happening. A couple of hours ago I was talking to my dad about chalupas. I wanted to go back to that moment and start the day all over again.

Richard sat down in an orange vinyl chair at the end of the hallway, now silent, but still seething. He stared straight ahead, picking his lip and tapping the heels of his feet up and down, up and down, like he was readying for a race. I ran into my mom's room, grabbed my cell phone and walked down a long hall to the adjacent wing of the hospital. I found a quiet visiting room and—pacing in front of the vending machines with hands trembling—dialed my sister Kristina in San Francisco.

My sister Kristina was ten years older than I was. My brother fourteen years older. I was the baby and—as my mom revealed to me one day on the air during an afternoon drive radio show I co-hosted in Los Angeles—a "mistake." She might have used the word "surprise" or "unplanned," but what I heard that day was "mistake." Shattering all previous notions that my parents had decided after a ten-year hiatus to make a go at a second family. I actually loved being the baby. Double-promoted in school with a full-ride scholarship to the Rhode Island School Of Design at sixteen, my sister was out of the house by the time I was six. My brother was finishing college and I really was like an only child. My parents doted on me and took me everywhere they went. I don't ever remember having a babysitter. I was spoiled, for sure, but loved every minute of my childhood. And, even in my late forties, I was still attached to my mom at the hip.

"Hi Lisa," Kristina said as she picked up the phone.

"Mother's going to die. She just told us she's stopping her dialysis and is going to die," I abruptly blurted out, now pacing in circles around a small table surrounded by four chairs, not bothering with formalities or small talk or even a return hello.

Kristina had just left my parents' house two days before. My mom had summoned her—just as she had summoned me—to fly home to help her around the house. She wanted assistance with paperwork and organizing and asked both of us—no *told* both of us—to fly to Michigan to lend a hand. This is something she had never requested of us before. Ever. Perhaps we should have been suspect of the request from the get-go. Or maybe she didn't even know herself why she was asking us both to fly out and come to her aid with little advance notice.

To my mom's credit, she never made us feel guilty for not visiting more often than we had. With jobs and life, not to mention the ridiculous price of airfare, Kristina and I didn't make it back home nearly as often as we should. Richard lived in Michigan with his wife Kathy, and was the primary caregiver to my parents. Something I'm sure he resented us for, but was too kind to ever say.

"Okay," my sister nonchalantly replied to the news.

"Okay? Just like that? Okay?"

"Well, what do you want me to say? I can't blame her. Can you? Did you look at her? She can't see, she can't walk, she can't sit up—let her go."

We were on the same page. All in favor, two. All opposed, one.

Kristina said she would fly in as soon as possible. I told her about Richard's opposition as I paced nervously in front of the vending machines, while cursing my brother for always having to be in charge. Always having to be right. Always having to be the spokesperson for the rest of us, when in fact, we were *all* our mother's children. We all had a legitimate say in her life. His age didn't automatically make him the boss of me. Or us. Or anything.

After I hung up with my sister, I called my Aunt Dolores—or Auntie Dee as we fondly call her. Auntie Dee is my mom's sister-in-law. She's the wife of my mom's late brother, Mike. But in our hearts, she is my mom's sister. She has always been like a second mother to me. I loved her as much as I loved my mom. Which is why I needed her so desperately at that moment.

My Uncle Mike—Auntie Dee's husband—died a couple of years earlier. This was a huge blow to my mom. He was her only sibling and the two of them were very close. He handled his last days much like my mom did. When he found out his prostate cancer had come back and metastasized, he decided to forgo treatment. So for approximately a year, Uncle Mike lived his life the way he wanted and saw his life thorough to the end on his terms. I admired that. It's ironic that—at the time—my mom didn't want my Uncle to stop his treatments. And then, at the end of her life, she was making the same decision he had. Obviously, she finally understood.

My Auntie Dee calmed me enough to compose myself and promised she would be at the hospital the following day.

"Just go into that room and be there for your mom. That's your job right now," Auntie Dee instructed.

And she was right. I had to go back to the room to see my mom, but dreaded the thought of dealing with my brother again. I was spent. As I headed back to my mom's wing and room 216, I saw a bearded figure dressed in a long black robe, holding a bible, walking toward her room. It was our parish priest.

He didn't.

He did.

My brother called the priest to have him come to the hospital to convince my mom that she shouldn't stop her treatments. Or so the story in my head was telling me. I conjured up a scenario in my mind and was convinced that he wanted the priest to tell my mom that this was *suicide* and that our church would not give her a proper burial if she decided to end her life. How. Dare. He.

My motherly instincts kicked in. Protecting my mother, as she would me, I ran down the hall in front of the priest and blocked my mom's hospital door. Yes, I was blocking a priest from going into my mom's room. Don't ask. Had anyone told me I'd do this even three hours earlier, I would have said they were nuts. One half of me wanted to cross myself and ask for forgiveness and the other half wanted to call security and have him removed. Looking back, I was admittedly out of line.

Father Milan, our parish priest, couldn't be kinder. He is a gentle man who loved my mother completely. He had been there for our family for years, and I'm sure on that day, was only there to bring comfort. But at the time my head was a hive-full of bees. Buzzzz, buzzzzzz . . . swatting away anything that would threaten my mom. It was a protective instinct. I didn't want anyone telling my mom that God disagreed with her decision and I was afraid that was what he was going to do.

My mom's neurologist intervened. Thank God. Yes, God. The same guy whose messenger I just nearly tackled to the ground. The neurologist took me down the hall as Father Milan entered my mom's room. I was being escorted down the hospital corridor by a neurologist. Awesome. I had officially been labeled crazy. I'm surprised they didn't alert the psych ward.

The neurologist took me to a small area with a couch and two chairs. He offered me a tissue, though the gesture didn't match his demeanor. A touchy-feely sort he was not. Burly, bearded and broad-shouldered, a little greasy in the forehead area, the guy barely smiled. After my display of absurdity, I wasn't expecting a laugh-fest, but I had hoped he might be a little bit more sympathetic to the situation and would somehow be on my side.

"Obviously," he said, with the same certainty one would have when describing the sky as blue or the grass as green, "your family has a lot of dysfunction."

O . . . M . . . G . . . did he just call us dysfunctional? Us? I could feel myself mentally aligning with my brother in solidarity, still seated in the orange chair down the hall. We were perfectly functional, or sane, or normal. Right? Weren't we? Wouldn't anyone chase a priest down a hall and practically tackle him in front of her mother's hospital room?

You, buddy, better watch your step. Or I'll tell my brother on you. Dysfunctional, my ass.

The neurologist talked to me for another ten minutes or so, but I didn't hear anything he had to say. All I heard was, "Dysfunctional, dysfunctional, dysfunctional, dysfunctional." That's all I retained. I looked up to see Father Milan standing in the doorway, looking toward me for a sign of approval to enter. Dr. Judgmental got up and Father Milan sat down.

"I want you to know I agree with what your mother has decided to do," he said in his thick, Serbian accent.

Oh boy, I really felt like an idiot. What should I have said at this point? Forgive me Father, for I have sinned? I can't help what I did, I'm dysfunctional—just ask the neurologist? Would you like a tissue? What should I have said after my display of nutcrackery?

"I'm sorry, Father Milan, I was just protecting my mother."

"I know you were."

"So you don't think she is committing suicide?"

"Suicide? No. That is not what we believe. That is not what I believe. Your Mother is ready to join the Father in heaven." He went on to say, "Would a person who stopped chemotherapy be committing suicide? Would a person who decided they didn't want to be kept alive by artificial means be committing suicide? No. If they are not actively taking their own life, it is not suicide. And in this case, your Mother is simply choosing to not be kept alive by machines."

"I'm sorry," I said again, my eyes cast downward focusing on the thumbnail I was picking to a bald stub. Hoping that if I just kept saying the words, "I'm sorry," they would erase the spectacle that had occurred a half-hour earlier.

We went on to talk about God and life and death and my mom. He told me how much he loved my mom and how sad that he, personally, was to see her go. He promised to stop by the house later in the week to visit my mom and give her her final sacrament. Final sacrament. Ugh.

This was really happening. My mom was going to die. It was time for the tissue. Where was Dr. Feelgood when I needed him?

I escorted Father Milan to the elevator and hugged him goodbye. I composed myself, wiped away the streaming eyeliner that had dried on my cheeks, and made my way back down the hall to room 216, doing my best not to run into the neurologist or any of the audience members who had witnessed our afternoon matinee of madness. I removed Angie from her carrier and placed her on the bed next to my mom. Angie nuzzled her head under my mom's hand saying, "pet me," while my mom continued to watch TV, oblivious to the passionate discourse that had been going on around her. My brother and I spoke few words the rest of the night. The wrangling settled into an unspoken, silent truce on both of our parts. We both needed to regroup before venturing into any further conversation. I knew that, eventually, everyone would come around to rally as our matriarch took her final bows. We had to. Millie would have it no other way.

Richard left the hospital first that evening. Saying goodbye to my mother he turned in my direction, but didn't acknowledge me as he exited through the door. Obviously still hurting, apparently, that I wasn't taking his side in this matter, I thought it best to remain silent and let him sit with his own thoughts overnight. We all needed to do that.

As my dad and I prepared to leave, my mom gave us a list of things she wanted us to have ready for her at home—along with some things she wanted us to bring her the following day: socks, her handheld slot machine game, a handful of hard candies and her purse.

Even in the end, a woman doesn't want to be without her purse. My grandmother—my mother's mom who we called Baba—lived with our family for the final decade of her life. She was reclusive and only left the house for family functions. But on a daily basis, not even getting out of her house coat, she would wake up, grab her purse, and walk into the family room to spend the day in her brown flowered upholstered chair, handbag at her side. When she would leave the room she'd take her purse with her. I never looked inside, but it was as if she had a million dollars in there and was reluctant to leave her riches anywhere in the house for fear that someone would take them. Either that, or it made her feel like she was actually going somewhere every day. Have purse, will travel. I often regretted not putting her purse in her casket with her. I'm sure its absence made her soul uneasy. So on this day, as my mom requested *her* handbag, I wanted to honor her wishes without question.

We took down her requests, kissed her goodnight and the three of us—my dad, Angie and I—headed back out into the cold and made our way to my parents' house, emptied from the day's events that had bull-dozed us all.

Death was exhausting. And day one was behind us. I desperately needed a nap to process it all.

Day 2

DECEMBER 12

"Away in a manger, no crib for a bed . . ."

Have you ever had one of those mornings where you wake up from a bad dream saying to yourself "Man, that was a horrible dream," only to realize it wasn't a dream, but was something that happened the day before? That's the kind of morning I was welcomed with today.

It was true. My mom was dying. And I really wasn't sure how to deal with that or reconcile my feelings. The initial plan for today—prior to my mother's fall, prior to her landing in the hospital—was supposed to be to take my parents to an independent living facility they were interested in moving to. My dad and brother had already been there, but my mom and I hadn't seen it yet. That was one of the reasons I was in Michigan for the weekend. We were going to look at their future home. The future. That thing that exists, not today, but tomorrow. That thing that my mom will no longer be a part of. Instead, I would be waiting for hospice to deliver a bed. A bed my mom would be dying in. In the future. Right there in the family room she had lived in for thirty-four years.

My Baba died in this same house my senior year of college, twenty-seven years earlier. I remember that morning so clearly. A hundred and fifty miles away, in a house on Main Street, I had been dreaming about playing my piano in our church gymnasium. The gymnasium had a raised stage with thick, green velvet curtains. I had performed many a show on this stage, in front of people sitting on folding chairs, with the church junior choir as a child. It's the first place I caught the entertainment bug. And the second place I kissed a boy. In my dream, as I played the piano, I saw my grandmother walking toward me on the stage. I could hear her slippers shuffling on the wood floor, echoing through the gym as she approached. She stopped in front of the piano, put her finger to her lips and said, "Shhhhh, I'm trying to sleep." So I played quieter and she walked off the stage, into the wings, disappearing into the darkness behind the green curtain. At the same moment the phone rang; it was my mom. She told me that my grandmother had died that morning. My mom woke up to find her mother lying in the hallway between her bedroom and the bathroom. We were never sure if she was coming or going, but either way that became her final resting place. My dream was my grandmother saying goodbye.

It took a very long time for my mom to be able to walk through that hallway without crying. After my Baba died, my mom got down on her hands and knees and scrubbed the carpet. She kept seeing my grandmother's phantom outline on the floor and tried everything to get rid of it. She even resorted to spraying bleach on the cobalt blue carpeting, hoping that would make the image disappear. It only left behind purple stains that could still be seen on the carpet, almost three decades later. Constant reminders of the spot where my mother's mother took her last breath. I wondered if one day I would be driven to the same manic scrubbing, but in the family room where my mom would soon be resting.

The bed would be arriving shortly and I had to move furniture around to make room for it. My dad and I lifted the coffee table from the center of the room and placed it behind the couch. This would end up serving as our supply closet. Our own little M.A.S.H. unit. The bed would sit where the coffee table had lived since my parents moved in. This was evidenced by the deep divots in the mauve pile carpeting. When vacuuming, the divots always made putting the table back in place easy. It was like a roadmap. I went into the basement and retrieved some extra bedding—something that would fit a twin bed. Pillows, sheets, blankets. *Lots* of blankets. My mom was always cold. I imagine when you're dying, you get even colder, so I piled them on to my arm and brought them upstairs.

I stacked the bedding on the couch and got dressed for the day. My mom was still in the hospital and most likely wouldn't be coming home until the following morning. She still had to have her dialysis port removed from her chest—which is a bigger production than it sounds—so she'd probably have to stay one more night for observation. Which, in theory, was a strange concept. She was going into hospice care to die. When the end goal is death, does it matter if one is observed or not?

The doorbell rang. The bed guys had arrived. I opened the door in the family room that led to the garage and reached around to push the button to open the garage door. As the door rolled up on its track, two men appeared carrying various parts of what would become my mom's final resting spot. They stepped through the door and laid the pieces on the floor of the now emptied family room, organizing them as they would be put together.

I laughed as I said, "I didn't know Ikea made hospital beds." The bed guys didn't laugh. I thought it was funny. Perhaps the joke would have gone over better in California. Or Sweden.

The metal bed would be sitting in the same location where Jenny and I made out with Ron and Ricky in high school the night that they snuck in during our sleepover, soaked from rain. While getting a hickey in the tenth grade on the floor in front of the TV, I never would have imagined that one day my mom would lie dying in that very same spot. It was all so surreal.

As one man began assembling the bed, another went out to the van to retrieve an oxygen machine and six tanks. A half-dozen tanks of oxygen? Would my itty bitty mom really need all of this to keep her comfortable for the next few days? It seemed so excessive. How much oxygen could one consume?

With the bed nearly complete, the delivery man removed a large vinyl raft-like contraption out of a sealed plastic bag. This inflatable mattress would take air in and out for the next two weeks, keeping my mom's blood circulating evenly so she wouldn't get bedsores. This would be one of the many lessons I'd learn about home hospital care, hospice and pharmaceutical disbursement in the coming days. Nursing 101. The gentlemen from the hospital supply company also gave us various tubes and pads, explaining what each was for and when we would need to use them. After a crash course in O_2 administration, we signed some papers and the delivery men left. My parents' cozy family room had—in less than an hour—been turned into a triage unit. I would never be able to look at their family room the same way again.

Once the delivery men were gone, my dad and I headed back to the hospital. With my dad in the pilot's seat, I watched memories pass by outside the car window, like scenes from a movie. Old friends' houses, restaurants, schoolyards, movie theaters—all of them had strong memories attached. This was my life in one thirty-five-minute drive. I just wished there was some way, on this day, I could rewrite the scene that was about to unfold.

"So how about that bed, Father? It's pretty fancy." I knew the bed in the middle of the family room made my dad sad. It was a tangible symbol of the finality that awaited us all. I tried to bring some levity to the situation.

"Yeah, it's something."

"Did you see how it raises up and down, and how the back can be raised so Mother can watch TV?"

My dad didn't respond. I knew somewhere in his head he thought maybe, just maybe, she would have a change of heart and not have to use the fancy Ikea-like hospital bed after all.

So I didn't bring it up again. I spent the rest of the trip silent, listening to my parents' favorite country station and trying to keep my mind off my mom's future. And my dad's driving.

We pulled into the hospital's parking lot and took the first handicapped spot available. This was one of the benefits of hanging out with an almost ninety-year-old: Prime parking. Especially appreciated when the winds were biting any piece of exposed skin on your body. After almost three days of coming and going, we had the routine down: Park, get badge, go up to room 216, talk to relatives, friends and doctors, force away tears when I looked at my mom, then go home. And that's exactly what we did this afternoon.

When we arrived in my mom's room, she was talking to her roommate, Valerie, through the curtain that separated them. Valerie was a beautiful, young African-American woman, in her late twenties or early thirties, with a husband who never left her bedside. Her husband, Damon, ran a home ambulance service for the elderly. They were a sweet and caring couple. Damon would often walk around the curtain to my mom's side of the room, sit by my mom's bedside and talk to her or say a prayer with her. My mom wasn't a particularly religious person but, smitten with Damon and his kindness, she would take his hand and let him lead her in prayer.

"He's so *handsome*, isn't he?" she'd say, in what she perceived to be a hushed voice, but was really loud enough for people to hear three rooms down. I think she had a little crush on Damon. And Damon couldn't have been a nicer and more caring friend for my mom during this time.

Occasionally, Damon and Valerie would open the curtain so everyone could mingle and talk to each other. But for the most part, the curtain was closed—their family on one side, our family on the other—both families praying that the women they loved would heal and get out of the hospital soon.

I didn't know the reason for Valerie's hospital stay but she had been in for over a month. Superficially she looked fairly healthy. She was thin, but not emaciated. Cancer, perhaps? Kidney disease like my mother? It was a mystery. My mom never knew, either. If they told her, she most likely didn't hear them or was loopy from her pain medicines and didn't comprehend. Whatever it was that kept Valerie in the hospital, it must have been something serious for an insurance company to allow a month-long stay. A hospital will toss you out an hour after giving birth, for goodness' sake. I thought it might be too personal to ask, so I just let it be.

"Hello," my dad and I said, as we walked past Valerie's bed toward my mom's side of the room. We had met the couple the evening before as we were leaving. They heard the fights. They witnessed the family feud. But they were kind enough to pretend they weren't listening through the cotton wall that separated us.

"Millie, your beautiful daughter and handsome husband are here!" said Valerie, enthusiastically.

"Send 'em in!" my mom instructed, as if Valerie was the gatekeeper to my mom's palace.

"The queen will see you now," said Valerie, waving her hand in a sweeping motion toward my mom's bed.

In two short days, Valerie and Damon had become extended family to my mom. It's a phenomenon that occurs in hospitals, airplanes and jury duty. I've left flights best friends with the person sitting next to me. Of course, the familiarity is short lived. You rarely keep in touch. But while you're immersed in it, an attachment develops and you think you'll be friends forever.

"Lisa, tell Valerie about your new job!" yelled my mom from the other side of the curtain, stretching out the word *jaaaaaahhhbb* in her hard Midwest accent.

I stopped at the foot of Valerie's bed, unsure of what I was supposed to say.

"Millie tells me you have a really important job in the music industry! And you used to work for *Playboy*? Come, sit here and tell me all about it! Do you know Whitney Houston? Do you know Hugh Hefner? Can I come visit you when I'm out of here?"

I laughed, and tapped Valerie on her foot, over the blanket that covered her. "Valerie, my mom sure has a way of talking me up!"

"Tell her, Lisa! Tell her about your new jaaaaaahhhbb! And the time you went to the Playboy Mansion!" wailed my mother, screeching out the word "maaaaaiiinchuun" with the same Midwest spirit.

"Mother, Valerie and Damon don't want us to bother them!"

"Oh baloney!" said my mom. "Stay over there and talk to Valerie for a while."

So I did. I told Valerie and Damon about my new job and my old jobs. They asked about people I knew, places I'd been, things I had seen. They wanted to know all about Hollywood and movie stars. You would have thought I was Julia Roberts or something. My mom had somehow elevated me to superstar status in my absence when, in reality, I had a desk job at a prestigious music awards show. I wasn't actually one of the people who *wins* the awards. But I humored them and tried to make my little life in Los Angeles as exciting as I could make it to try to match the Lisa my mom created.

It was nice to know my mom was proud of me. I have a feeling that no matter what I chose to do in my life, she'd still make me the superstar of whatever chosen career I landed in.

When I was finished regaling Valerie and Damon with tales of far-off lands, I walked over to my mom's side of the room and sat with her on her bed. She was in particularly good spirits today, despite the fact that she was slated to die. Perhaps that's why she was in such a good mood. She no longer had to worry about the pain or her back or who was going to take her to her dialysis appointments. A levity enveloped her and I, for one, was not going to do anything to tilt the scale.

"Mother, you should see your bed at home! It's very high-tech!"

"Oh, that's so nice!"

"And it's right in the middle of the family room so you can watch all of your stories and look out the window into the backyard."

My mom smiled, staring at the TV on the wall. That is, what she could see of the picture, with her cataracts and macular degeneration. I watched my mom watch the TV. Angie fell asleep at her feet. My dad stood at the window, gazing out into the unknown.

I had been thinking a lot about the dying process since the news was delivered to us the day before. The way I figured it, there were three ways to die. First, the "he dropped dead on the golf course" way, where one minute you're here, the next, you're not. You're forty-five-years-old, the father of two small children and one day the good Lord just decides to take you. People are shocked, they say things like, "I can't believe he's *gone*. I mean, I just talked to him *yesterday*." "He was so healthy. He was a *runner*. How could he *die*?" People always glorify this way of dying, saying that "If I die, I just want to go in my sleep." Or, "He was lucky he didn't suffer." Dropping dead on the golf course has never appealed to me. It wouldn't be my number one choice.

I'd prefer the second choice. The "You have less than a year to live," prognosis. This is the one I most gravitate toward. I think it's the Virgo in me that is drawn to the possibility of being able to organize before you go. It's the death that gives you a while to tie up loose ends, get your papers in order, say your goodbyes, have a garage sale. It's the death that allows you some closure. Enough time to spend your final days appreciating life, maybe quit your job, travel a little, but not too much time to sit around with a chronic illness that will cause you pain. It seems to me to be the best way to go.

Then finally, there's the way my mom would be going, which is wedged right in the middle of the golf course death and the year to live death.

When my mom told us she was stopping dialysis, I wasn't sure exactly what that meant in terms of how long she'd have to live. She had just started dialysis a month earlier. She had lived eighty-five years without it, perhaps she could live a year or two if she stopped. My mom's doctor, who stopped by to check on my mom, informed us that it would be a maximum of two weeks until my mom's kidneys went into complete failure. Fourteen days. That was all. Less than a month. I suppose it's not as bad as dropping dead in an instant, but it doesn't seem like a whole lot of time to gather ye rosebuds before you head out.

My mom didn't seem to be bothered by it. Fourteen days was just fine with her.

"I'm happy you're here," my mom said, lovingly, as she stroked my hand resting atop her lap.

"Me too, Mother. Me, too."

We watched TV for a few hours. Chatted about life. My mom was very worried about me taking two weeks off work. She was so proud of my new job and didn't want me to do anything to jeopardize it. She had me text my boss to have her reassure my mother that my job would still be waiting for me when I returned home.

"Yes, you will still have a job," texted my boss, urging me to not think about the office and just concentrate on my mom for the coming weeks. I showed the text to my mom. Of course, she couldn't actually see the words on the phone, but the light and shadows were enough to convince her that my job would be okay and still be waiting for me when I returned to California. That gave my mom one more mark on the peace side as she tidied for her exit.

My mom dictated tasks to me that she wanted to take care of in the next two weeks. From paying the property taxes to getting legal documents in shape, my mom wanted to make sure everything was in order before she left. I don't think she would have died until it was.

Doctors came in and out throughout the day. Some performing checkups, others talking to her in private making sure she knew the gravity of the step she was about to take. Any time a doctor would ask her to examine the decision she was making, she would get visibly agitated.

"I know what I'm doing! Just let me *go*!"

And with that, the doctors would pat her on the arm, or grab her hand and say, "Well, okay then, we'll do all that we can to help you 'go' in comfort."

After a full day of visiting, I could see my mom wanted to sleep. We told her we were leaving and that she would be in good hands in our absence. Not only did she have a hospital full of doctors and nurses at her disposal, but her neighbors Valerie and Damon were just a few feet away, there for my mom should she need anything.

As I kissed my mom goodnight, I told her that I'd see her the next morning at home. The thought of returning home to her beloved family room and TV made her very, very happy.

Day 3

"Bring us some figgy pudding . . ."

Now that I knew I would be staying in Michigan for an indefinite amount of time, I had to do some shopping for incidentals I'd need over the coming weeks. After all, I only packed for a three-day trip. Shampoo, face wash, razors and perfume—I would need all of these things in the coming days. While my dad made calls to family and friends to tell them news of my mom's fate, I headed to the neighborhood grocery store.

Grocery shopping in my hometown was always more festive, for some reason, than shopping back in Los Angeles. Food always tasted better at my mom's house than it did at my own. An egg and cheese fried in a pan at my mom's could conjure up childhood memories and love and kisses and comfort. The same egg and cheese in L.A. was just that: an egg and some cheese. Was it the magic of the house? The magic of my mom's pans? Or just the magic of a mom being around to make everything Technicolor?

My mom's answer was butter. Lots and lots of butter.

As I strolled down the aisles, I filled my basket with Lean Cuisine, fruit, cereal and Faygo pop. In Michigan, we didn't call soda "soda." We called it pop. A hard habit to break once I moved to California, where people from the Golden State would stare at you like you were speaking German when you asked for a "pop" with your fries. Faygo was my heroin. And I'd need plenty of my soothing nectar in the days to come.

As I rounded the corner in the produce section, the smell of flowers filled the air. My mom was never big on flowers in general. She didn't garden. She didn't have any live plants in her house. And when someone would send her flowers for a birthday or Mother's Day, she would always say, "Why did you spend your money on flowers? They're just going to die. You should save your money. I don't need flowers." Of course, we still bought her flowers. Deep down I know she loved them. But, somehow, I think she never felt worthy of their beauty

I learned the hard way not to ever buy my mom lilies. The fragrant flower was one of my favorites. I always said that if I had a daughter, I'd name her Lily. That is, until my mom cursed the name with one of her many superstitions. One year for my mom's birthday, I sent her a Hawaiian-inspired bouquet filled with gardenias, tuberose, plumeria and lilies. When she called to thank me for the flowers she said, ". . .but don't ever send me lilies again. Those are the death flower. Lily means someone died. I don't want lilies." Duly noted. I never bought her a lily again. And my name of choice, for my future baby girl if I ever had one, changed to Ruby—a homage to my maternal grandmother. I never told my mother for fear she'd somehow jinx it.

So at this time of my mom's life—even though a lily or two would be appropriate considering the circumstances—I decided to go with her favorite flowers, white roses. I scooped up every bouquet of white roses they had. I even took a few mixed bouquets to pick the white roses out, and place the remaining flowers elsewhere in the house. I wanted the sights, sounds and smells of her final days to be filled with everything she loved the most. Of this, she was worthy.

When I returned home from the store, I put away the groceries and filled assorted vases and glasses and small bowls with water, placing the trimmed rose stems in the vessels. I encircled my mom's bed with the bouquets, placing them on the TV, the table next to my mom's bed, at her feet, behind her head, to the left of her and on the fireplace. I wanted her to see white roses in any direction she turned. And I wanted her to smell white roses even past the point she couldn't smell roses any more.

The stage was now set for my mom's arrival.

At 10:15 a.m. the doorbell rang. It was the ambulance drivers who transported my mom back home. This would be her final ride and the last time outside air would fill her lungs. I went back into the family room, surveyed the area, fluffed her pillows once more and opened the door to the garage. The drivers wheeled my mom past my dad's Jeep Liberty, then lifted her up over the threshold into the house. They placed the gurney next to her bed then lifted her frail body off the gurney and onto the hospital bed, where she would remain for the next two weeks. We signed some paperwork and they were on their way.

The countdown had officially begun.

"Awwww, it's good to be home." The voice coming out of my mom's mouth was familiar, but unfamiliar at the same time. A weakened version of that I once knew, but still with the rasp that was so identifiable and loved and imitated by everyone who knew her.

"We sure are happy to have you here! This house isn't the same without you, Mother."

My mom looked around the room and smiled. "The roses are beautiful, my darling."

"Can you see them?" I asked, not sure if her cloudy eyes could make out the white bouquets surrounding her.

She closed her eyes and took in a deep inhalation, her lips turning up at the corners in a half smile. The bones underneath the purple bruise on her chest got more pronounced as her rib cage rose and fell. "I can smell them."

I filled my mom in on the bed's operation, the oxygen administration and all of the pads and wipes and lotions and brushes she would be using over the coming days. I would be her nurse. She, my patient. She looked relaxed and relieved. I turned on her beloved television, raised the back of her bed so she could see the screen and the two of us sat there, silent, soaking in this new reality. We would do our best to make her comfortable during her transition.

The head hospice nurse, Nancy, stopped by for her initial visit shortly after my mom arrived home. She walked us all through the process, explained what the next couple of weeks would entail, told us what we would experience and prepared my mom for her final days. My mom nodded her head as if she understood the gravity of what was happening. But I was never quite sure if she was fully aware of the outcome.

I was perplexed as to how someone could remain so calm knowing that in a few days they would be dead. But she placidly continued to nod her head as Nancy gave us the rundown. She went through the list of hospice members who would be visiting in the coming days, as well, and what their roles would be in my mom's forthcoming farewell. There was quite a crew: nurses, aides, social workers, even priests. Hospice prepares the dying patient, and family, so thoroughly that there are few questions in the end.

My mom had a way of endearing herself to everyone who came in contact with her. She was funny, open and brutally honest. Wherever my mom went, she made friends. When I first moved to Los Angeles, I was asked to be a guest on the *Leeza Gibbons Show* for a segment they were doing on following your dreams. They had asked my parents to be a part of the panel, as well. My mom stole the show. By the end of the hour, Leeza was an official member of the Millie Goich Fan Club. You just couldn't help loving her. She was that charismatic.

After Nancy, the hospice nurse, finished her instructional tour, my mom interjected a non-sequitur, "Are you married, Nancy?"

"Yes, I am, Millie," responded Nancy with a smile on her face.

"Good. You should be," said my mom authoritatively, as if her word were gospel. "You're nice."

"You're nice, too, Millie," replied Nancy. Her round face exuding comfort and her gentle touch sending assurance through my mother's deteriorating body.

And with that, the two of them solidified their friendship, a loving relationship that would continue for the next eleven days.

Hospice nurses are a rare and treasured breed. To be able to give your heart freely to a patient knowing that the connection is so short lived, is truly a special trait. The gift they bring to those at the end of their own lives is priceless. It's a profession that deserves more accolades than it receives.

One of the rules of hospice was that my mom was to no longer take any further medications to prolong her life. Nancy asked to have access to my mom's medications so she could package them up. The rounding up of my mom's meds looked like a drug bust in an episode of *Cops*. My parents' kitchen cupboard was like a pharmacy. My dad's meds on the left, my mom's on the right. Generic white bottles lined three shelves they shared with the fine china we used at every holiday gathering. How they even knew what was what and what drug took care of what ailment was incomprehensible. Every morning they would divvy up that day's pills. My mom always took hers with water from her pink *World's Greatest Grandma* coffee mug. The cup was stained brown inside from years of coffee she had never quite gotten clean. After she and my dad took their pills, they'd take their blood pressure, document it and my dad would conclude the morning ritual with a prick of his finger to test his blood sugar levels. A free clinic right there in the kitchen on Newport Drive. Every morning. Same routine.

But on this day, one half of the cupboard was cleared out. The meds were placed into two large boxes and moved into my mom's bedroom with strict instructions not to touch them and to no longer administer them to my mother, regardless of any symptoms she'd be experiencing in the coming days. We were no longer in living mode. We were in dying mode. And her old pills were for the living.

These drugs were exchanged for the hospice comfort kit, also known as the emergency kit, e-kit or hospice kit. I called it "The Box." This was a small box of meds that would sustain my mom throughout the coming days and address any emergencies that might arise. The contents of this box would help alleviate the inevitable symptoms of pain, anxiety, nausea, insomnia and breathing problems. Lorazepam for anxiety, Atropine to treat wet respirations (also known as the "death rattle"), Haloperidol to treat agitation and terminal restlessness, Compazine for nausea and vomiting, Dulcolax for constipation, and finally, Morphine for the end pain that precedes death.

The Box would remain in the refrigerator—untouched—for almost two weeks. It was something we ignored, pretending it never existed. Shoving it further to the back, behind the cheese and deli trays, the leftover ham and potatoes. If it wasn't there, we wouldn't have to use it. And if we didn't use it, it would mean my mom was still alive and well.

When Nancy left, I sat with my mom in what would be our last moments alone together before family and friends started filling my parents' house. I couldn't stop staring at her. Her eyes were focused on the TV and I sat by her side.

She turned toward me and said, "Look what I learned at the hospital."

"What?"

"Give me your hand. Make a fist."

I extended my arm out in a fist. She did the same and bumped my fist with hers.

I laughed. "Where did you learn that?"

"An aide in the hospital taught it to me. It's called a fist bump."

"Yes it is," I chuckled.

"He said, 'around here, we don't say goodbye, we say, see ya later.' And then you fist bump."

From that point forward, my mom fist bumped everyone who came through our house for the last weeks of her life. She would tell the story over and over again as if she'd never told it before. She never said goodbye to anyone who left in those two weeks. Only a "see ya later!" The aide had no idea what traction his lesson would receive.

❄

The doorbell rang about a half hour later. It was the first of many visitors who came bearing love, stories, laughter and food for this woman we all loved so much.

Food, glorious food. The food was a godsend during those fourteen days. Food is the best gift anyone could give to a grieving family. It sustains a family in so many ways. When one is caregiving, there is no time to cook. There is barely time to eat. Something as simple as a salad can fill hearts, bellies and souls.

My mom loved the company. She welcomed a steady stream of visitors on her first day home—nieces, nephews, grandchildren, friends—and covered the same bases with each of her guests, which would become a script of sorts during her two-week going-away party:

1. Did you eat?

2. Didn't we have fun when we (fill in the blank)?

3. Will you come to my picnic in heaven when you get there?

4. I'll miss you when I go 'up there.'

5. Take something with you when you leave.

Inspired by a nurse's suggestion while in the hospital, my mom took her goodbyes a step further. She wanted to make videos for those she loved so she would be remembered when she was gone. When guests were sitting at her bedside, she put on her director's hat and instructed me to get my phone and start taping her message. Holding the person's hand, she looked into the camera and gave them her final words of fare-well. Never was there a dry eye during these recordings.

"I hold you in my heart," she began. "I will hold you there forever. Don't forget me. I know, once in a while you will think of me. I have been so blessed with so many good friends, and I will never, ever forget you. I will see you somewhere along the line. I will see you." It was diffi-cult to see my telephone screen through my tears.

This message was repeated several times over the next eleven days as family and friends occupied the special seat, and my mom, like Steven Spielberg, set the scene for her next blockbuster. "Open the curtains.

Give me a little more light. Take off your coat. Sit on my left. Look at the camera. Hold my hand. There. That's perfect." Lights. Camera. Action.

My mom loved making the videos. She was a ham at heart. My dad, on the other hand, was unable to sit in the room when my mom was leaving her messages. At one point, he got so angry he yelled, "Goddammit, stop taping! Just stop!" He couldn't bear to hear her say goodbye one more time. I couldn't blame him. To this day, he hasn't looked back on his own. And I haven't had the heart to encourage it.

In addition to videographer, I took on a new responsibility. Caregiver. For the first time in my life, the tables were turned. The mother-child role reversed. My mom's life was now in my hands. Unable to do anything for herself—from the simplest task of rolling on her side, to the more complicated issues of relieving herself and cleaning herself afterward—these jobs were now my responsibility. They weren't assigned to me, by any means. I just naturally picked them up. Without question. You just step into gear when nature calls. This must have been how she felt with me when I was a baby. We got into a rhythm. This would be my privilege until the moment my mom took her last breath. As long as I was around, she didn't have to worry. It wasn't without its frustrations, though. She and I had to work to find a comfortable space where she was allowed to let herself go and I would be trusted to catch her.

As my mom's first day home wound down, and the house emptied, my dad and I cleaned the kitchen, locked the doors, and tucked my mom in for her first hospice sleep in the house.

"Goodnight Mother, I love you," I said as I wiped my hand across her forehead.

"I love you so much," she said as she patted my arm that rested atop her belly. "Why don't you go play the piano for a while?" she asked.

"We don't have the piano anymore, Mother. You gave it away."

"Oh," she said, forgetting for a moment that the piano was no longer in the house.

"Why did you ever quit piano?" she continued.

"The same reason I quit violin and ballet, Mother. Boys."

"That was dumb," she said.

"Amen."

"You were so good."

"I was never really *that* good at any of them."

"I don't agree."

"Let's face it, I was never going to be a prima ballerina with my short, stubby legs."

"But you and Teddy could have been a team," referring to my piano-playing husband who regularly tours with major acts and makes his living as a musician.

"Oh, just what he'd want, Mother. A regular Lucy and Ricky."

"I liked that show," she mused. "You still shouldn't have quit."

Once her eyes had closed, I retired to my childhood bedroom with my old books, photographs and stuffed animals to comfort me. My dad fell asleep on the couch next to my mom that evening, sliding his hand between the metal rails of her bed to hold hers, something he hadn't let go of for sixty-four years. He would remain there for the next ten nights.

Day 4

"On the fourth day of Christmas my true love gave to me
four Calling Birds, three French Hens, two Turtle Doves
and a Partridge in a Pear Tree . . ."

My sister Kristina arrived in Michigan today from San Francisco. Kristina, ten years my senior, would become the night shift to my day shift, the room service attendant to my nurse, the yin to my yang. We seamlessly traded tasks and leaned on each other during the coming days. I couldn't have gotten through this without her.

After my mom arrived home, we were in hunker down mode. Normally, when visiting my parents, I'd spend my days with them shopping or visiting relatives and my evenings out with old friends. But this visit was unexpectedly different.

This day began like every other day in this fourteen-day period, and all days would begin the same. Every morning, my sister, or I—whichever one of us woke up first—went into the family room to see if my mom was still breathing. It sounds morbid, but, not knowing what to expect with this death thing, it just became part of our routine. Whether or not my mom was breathing and alive wasn't easy to discern, even in her healthier days. Throughout my mom's life, when she slept, it always looked like she was dead. Her wrinkled eyelids would fuse closed and her mouth, lips glued together, would turn down into a frown. We joked about it. My nephew once took a photo of my mom sleeping in bed, with my dad at her side making an exaggerated sad face. My mom laughed to the point of tearing when she saw the photo, having no idea how she looked when she was asleep.

"Oh my *gaaahhhddd*, I look *awful!*" she'd say, unable to catch her breath.

That photo always made me laugh. And it made her laugh. And I still laugh when I think about it today. And that picture was what I thought about every morning I conducted the "is she breathing?" check, walking into the family room, staring at the blanket covering my mom's stomach, knowing that if I saw movement, we were in the clear for that day.

Today we were in the clear.

Once my mom was awake, I turned on the television. My parents had their TV running from morning until night. Neither could hear that well, so the TV was always turned up to near maximum, ear-splitting volume. In her final couple of years, my mom's macular degeneration was so bad that she couldn't see the TV unless she was sitting right on top of it. She loved the morning news shows, her "stories," the evening news, *Wheel of Fortune* and cop dramas like *CSI* and *Cold Case*. Days weren't determined by the calendar, but by what was on TV.

And Lifetime movies. Oh, did my parents love Lifetime movies. They gravitated toward the formulaic plots and battered-woman-turned-hero story lines. After getting in the groove of watching them, it's difficult to watch a good film without feeling out of rhythm somehow. I would bring screening copies of Oscar-nominated movies home from work and my mom and dad would scoff.

"Is Melissa Gilbert in this movie?"

"No Mother, she isn't."

"Oh," she'd say, unable to hide the disappointment in her voice. "That's okay. We'll watch it anyway."

My mom also had a great love of radio. I'm fairly certain that's what inspired me to be an on-air personality. When the TV wasn't on—and even sometimes when it was—my mom had the radio going. She loved to play radio contests. She won all sorts of things during her lifetime: movie tickets, gift certificates, trips and—her biggest prize—the $10,000 jackpot in the Q *Crystal Ball*. She painstakingly high-lowed a twelve-digit number over the course of a month until that fateful day when the DJ said, "When you hear us play *That's The Way I Like It,* call in with the twelve-digit number and win the jackpot!" She won. The money was used to move the family out of Detroit and into the suburbs. Her name was plastered all over the city: bus posters, newspaper ads, TV commercials and even those little cards they used to have sitting on the counter at record stores that listed the weekly Top 100. *Millie Goich of Detroit Wins $10,000 in the Q-Crystal Ball!* Her fifteen-minutes of fame had been realized.

But this morning, it was only the TV that kept her ears occupied. And next on the morning's schedule was potty and clean-up time. These were the most difficult of all of the tasks. The first few days home, my mom was still using the toilet to relieve herself. We had a portable toilet that we would pull up to the side of my mom's bed. Raising the back of her bed to the upright position, my sister and I would gently swing her legs over the side of the bed then lift her fragile body out of bed and onto the toilet, carefully trying not to get her nightgown soiled or break any of her bones. She was so thin, with no muscle left on her frame, you could feel her bones crack in your hands when holding her in your arms. Getting her out of bed was difficult. She couldn't stand on her own, was extremely weak, and relied solely on us to get her on and off and back into bed at least four times a day. This was a humiliating process for my mom and not one that any of us enjoyed. Mostly her. Defecating in your own family room isn't something anyone thinks they'll ever have to do. But it was reality. And it's amazing what humans are capable of doing when the going gets tough.

You don't realize what you're made of, until a loved one is dependent on you. It's then that your true self shines. While my sister held the back of my mom's nightgown up and away from the toilet and I held my mom's arm, my mom—with barely any food or liquid in her stomach—would strain each morning to clear her body of the toxins that were building up now that her kidneys were functioning at almost zero. She would try to clean herself, but had no strength to do it properly. When she was finished I would take baby wipes and clean her, just as she did me when I was an infant. My sister and I would then put her clothes back on and my dad and I—or my sister and I—would lift her back into bed and cover her up until the next time we'd have to go through this ignominious undertaking.

Parent/Child care giving begins in the womb. A mother gently strokes her own belly to soothe her baby's restlessness, watching what she eats and staying away from anything that might harm her child. When the baby is born, it's a 24/7 vigil of care—swaddling, diapering, anticipating cries and deciphering what they mean, feeding, cleaning, keeping their child comfortable, happy and healthy.

Parenting doesn't stop when the child is able to care for themselves. As my mom once told me, "I'm going to worry about you and take care of you until the day I die, so get used to it!" And she did. Until she couldn't care for me any longer and it was suddenly my turn to care for her.

The day the roles reverse is foreign. It's a clumsy dance of love and responsibility, not wanting to cross any lines of respect. It's honoring this person who gave their life to you—not to mention literally gave you life—and taking their fragile body in your hands like a newborn, tending to their every need.

This would take some getting used to.

Breakfast followed. My mom wasn't eating much in these final days and was shrinking by the second. If we were lucky, she would eat three spoonfuls of oatmeal. We'd leave the bowl at her bedside hoping she would want more later. But she never did. Again, when the end result is death, forcing someone to eat doesn't become a priority.

After breakfast, the hospice workers visited, one after another— the nurse, the chaplain, the social worker, the caregiver. No part of my mom—from her head to her toes to her soul—went untended. Today my mom had an hour-long conversation with a Catholic chaplain. We weren't Catholic, but he came with the hospice deal. They talked about family and my mom's past, life and death.

This was followed by a visit from Father Milan—a two for one God deal today—as my mom prepared herself spiritually for her journey. Fortunately, it seemed, Father Milan didn't mention my breakdown from a couple of days prior. I guess it's all part of the confession mechanism priests come automatically equipped with. I just smiled an extra friendly, "See, I'm not dysfunctional!" smile as I walked him through the kitchen, down into the family room to my mom's bedside. I took his coat and hung it on the rack in the kitchen and asked him if he wanted anything to drink.

"Tea, Father Milan? Coffee?"

"No thank you. I'm fine," he replied, giving me a thumbs up, then turning his attention back to the patient.

My mom loved Father Milan, and I think the feeling was mutual. He called her Milka, the Serbian name for Millie. She called him Father.

Over the years, he had seen both my parents through cancer, my nieces through their baptisms and weddings and, now, was here for my mom to issue her last communion.

When my mom was diagnosed with a tumor in her colon seven years earlier, Father Milan had come to the hospital to visit her. My mom, still loopy from anesthesia, began to grill the priest on the importance of colonoscopies.

"Have you had a colonoscopy, Father Milan?" she asked.

My eyes popped open, as I swung my head in my mom's direction, uncomfortable at the thought of talking to the priest about something so personal.

"Mother . . ." I began to interrupt, trying to tell her to change the subject or not head in the direction she was heading.

"Whaaaaaat?" she snapped. "You don't think Father Milan has a colon? He has a colon and he poops just like you and me."

Oh God. She didn't.

Father Milan just laughed, knowing that the combination of my mom's no-holds-barred personality and the drugs, made for a frank discussion he wasn't afraid to engage in.

Today's visit was a little more somber. No talk of colons or bodily functions, but instead, subjects that fell within the priest's purview.

Though I sat in the kitchen to give them privacy, I could hear bits of their conversation from across the room.

"What happens when I die, Father?" she asked the bearded priest in his formal robes, sitting at her side.

"Well, I believe we go to heaven," he said, holding her hands and never taking his eyes off hers.

"Me too," she said with a certainty I had never heard in her voice prior to this when talking about life after death. Somehow she now knew that this was an ultimate destination.

"Will we have a party when I get there?" my mom asked, hoping for a yes, but bracing for a possible no.

"Of course! Everyone will be there to greet you and you'll have a big party! Like no other party you've ever had before. It will be in a meadow with the greenest grass you've ever seen. The flowers will be vibrant, the air will be fresh. And you, you sweet Milka, will be able to enjoy all of it free of pain. In a body that knows no sickness or disease."

My mom closed her eyes and smiled. The thought of a heaven party pleased her. And she nodded her head knowingly at the future.

Father Milan then proceeded to tell her a dream he had once about heaven that he was sure was affirmation that it did, indeed, exist. My mom was wide-eyed, like a child listening to someone reading an adventure story.

Before he left, my mom asked Father Milan to take a picture with her. He leaned over her bed, the heavy cross around his neck, swinging on its chain, clanking against the rails of the bed. My mom said we would send him the picture so he could remember her forever. He said, "Milka, you are one person I could never forget."

After Father Milan left, a steady stream of people stopped by to pay their respects to my mom. She truly held court like a queen from her hospital bed in the middle of her family room, only a few inches away from her former spot at the end of the couch. It's an enviable way to exit.

❄

Among today's guests were my Godmother Dorothy and one of her five daughters, Susan. My mom's friendship with my "Kuma" Dorothy (Kuma is a title given to godparents in the Serbian Orthodox Church) had sustained for as long as my parents' marriage. Kuma Dorothy and my mom brought out the funny in each other. And today's visit—despite the reason—wasn't any different. Kuma Dorothy was ninety-four going on forty-five. Walking five miles a day, taking dance lessons and sporting a face that would make Dorian Gray envious, she was the polar opposite of my mom who hadn't walked five miles in the past ten years. But the two of them were sisters at heart. And with Kuma Dorothy lying in one direction across the couch, and my mom facing in the other in her hospice bed, six hours of laughter ensued. They were like twelve-year-old girls at a pajama party.

For old time's sake, I asked my mom to re-tell one of my favorite stories of an afternoon drive with my Kuma Dorothy and her daughters, Carol and Lynne, along with my Aunt Margaret in the summer of 1962, when my mom was only a couple of months away from giving birth to me. I knew it would be the last time my mom would tell the story and I needed to hear it in her voice, so I could store it in my heart for future reference.

"It was June of 1962, wasn't it Dorothy?" asked my mom, looking over at her friend who had her feet folded over the back of the couch.

"It was summer, I know that," said Dorothy, squinting her eyes as if she was looking at a calendar page from fifty years earlier.

"Your Aunt Margaret, Kuma Dorothy, Carol, Lynnie and I were in your father's old Chevy. Remember that car, Nick?"

"Yep. I remember," said my dad, not looking up from the *Time* magazine he was reading, having heard this story probably no less than twenty-five times over the past fifty years.

"Carol and Lynnie were still kids at the time. I was driving. I still drove in those days, you know. I was going to drop the girls off at their house on Mapleridge. We were driving down Salter, got to Mapleridge and I put my foot on the brake to stop in front of their house and said, 'What the shit?' Nothing happened. The goddamned car wouldn't stop. I started to panic."

"I told her to put on her emergency brake," said Kuma Dorothy.

"Which didn't work!" added my mom. "It was frozen when I tried to pull it up. So I yelled to Dorothy and Margaret . . ."

"Hang your feet out the door!" interjected, Kuma Dorothy. "She wanted us to put our feet out the door like Fred Flintstone!"

"And the dummies listened to me!" laughed my mother, tears streaming down her face.

"We never listened to you, Millie! Your mom couldn't stop the car, so she turned the car up the alley to try to slow it down which was a smart move on her part. There were holes in the floor of your mom's car and we could see the gravel speeding by underneath the car," added Dorothy. "The girls were in the back seat screaming."

Laughing uncontrollably now, my mom continues, "Now your Aunt Margaret—who you know was a nun—was in the backseat with the kids praying on her rosary, 'Oh, dear God. Oh, dear Jesus.' I said, 'God and

Jesus aren't gonna stop this car, Margaret, get your feet out the door with Dorothy and help me stop this thing!'"

"She closed her eyes and flew down the alley without looking!" cackled Dorothy. "She didn't look! She just went straight through!"

"And then we stopped! I think Margaret's prayers worked because we didn't hit a goddamned thing and no one was hurt. But God that was funny," laughed my mom through tears.

Fortunately—for these two women who were still sitting together telling the story today, Dorothy's daughters, my Aunt Margaret who had passed away about twenty years earlier, and me, who was almost fully baked in my mom's belly at the time of the incident—there were no cars coming down the alley as the Chevy slowly rolled to a stop. From that day forward, my mom vowed never to drive again. A promise she held for nearly eighteen years. And my Aunt Margaret and Kuma Dorothy vowed never to listen to my mom during an emergency.

My mom was a worrier. Even on her deathbed, in her last days, she worried about everything. And the worry that was on her mind today were her "papers."

"Nick, go in the basement and get the big box," she ordered my dad, after my godmother and her daughter had left for the day.

"The Big Box" (not to be confused with the hospice comfort kit) was a fireproof gray, rusted container my parents kept in the basement, under the stairs, in a crawl space behind a locked door. The box contained everything from insurance policies to banking information to the title for the house. She wanted to make sure everything was in place and signed before she went. She couldn't rest easy until it was. She enlisted my cousin Bob, a lawyer, to go over all of her insurance papers, will and legal documents, and my Aunt Dolores to help organize her files. She insisted my dad drive to the post office that day to pay the house taxes that weren't due until the summer—six months away. My dad obediently agreed. She had me sit with her as she dictated a list of her belongings she wanted me to give to people.

"Would you give Sara that little bluebird pin off my jacket? I want Sara to take it." Sara is my niece—my mom's first granddaughter and my brother's daughter—who is a doctor. "I just want to give her something that'll remind her of one of her patients who really loved her. I think it's nice to leave something behind."

"Bluebird for Sara," I wrote on my list.

I cried. She continued, "Oh, and those angels that I bought for Vicki and Dolores, my God, they're one of a kind! Make sure you give them the angels."

"I'll give them the angels, Mother."

"And find Nicole a jacket. Something that will look cute on her. She always liked my sweaters and jackets. Make sure you take a few for her before you give everything to Goodwill." Nicole was Sara's younger sister and my mom's second granddaughter.

"I'll find her something cute."

This went on until my mom couldn't speak any longer. She gave away necklaces and earrings, pins and dishes. Family mementos she no longer needed would find a home among the living. Everyone left with a door prize when they visited my mom during those fourteen days.

My mom had actually begun this purge a few years earlier. It was the year she purchased the shredder. It was either an *Oprah* episode, or *60 Minutes* that scared her into thinking no piece of mail should ever be dumped into her garbage in one piece. So every day, she and my dad would bring the mail into the back bedroom where their new shredder lived and demolish the address into obscurity. As anyone who has shredded knows, it can be addicting. You can't just stop with mail. She began unearthing boxes in the basement, old files, photographs, junk drawer remnants—anything she could get her hands on. Once there was nothing left to shred, she began unloading contents of cupboards and drawers.

"If you want something, get it now, or I'm throwing it out." All four-feet-nine-inches of her on a mission.

I had taken a couple of things that meant a lot to me on previous visits—the wedding cake topper from my parents' wedding, an old metal box my mom used to keep in her bedroom and a piece of art that hung in her hallway.

I didn't know just how serious my mom was about the purge until I came to visit one weekend and saw that almost the entire house had been emptied out. Including the majority of my mom's antiques she had been collecting for years.

"Where's the china cabinet? And the table? The artwork in the basement? Where's that painting of the monastery that hung over the TV? Where did everything go?"

"I told you if you wanted it, take it, or I was getting rid of it."

"But where did it *go*?"

"I had an antique dealer come over and buy the stuff from me."

This didn't sound good. I hated even asking the next question, but ...

"How much did he give you for everything, Mother?"

"It doesn't matter. It's gone."

"How much?"

"$800."

I tried my best not to react or make my mom feel like she had done something wrong. But $800 would hardly scratch the surface of what those antiques were really worth. Sure, we should have taken the reins years ago and had someone come to the house for an appraisal. But we didn't. And she warned us. And here we were now with an empty house and nothing to show for the priceless antiques that were no longer up for grabs.

So much for an inheritance.

Cleaning helped stop the worry. She just couldn't stop worrying. Not about her upcoming death, but about the welfare of everyone else around her and how life would go on once she was gone. Everything needed to be in place and everyone needed to be taken care of and happy, before she could even fathom leaving this Earth behind.

I could appreciate the organization.

She'd always been this way. An incessant worrier. During a child-hood vacation to Pennsylvania she had a meltdown. I was in the back seat of the cobalt blue Chrysler Cordoba with the fine white Corinthian leather interior. We were styling as we cruised down the Pennsylvania

Turnpike. For the heck of it—I'm not sure why—I reached over into the front seat and pushed the button to the garage door opener. I was a kid. I was bored. It looked like something fun to do. My mom freaked out thinking that I opened the garage door . . . from Pennsylvania.

"Why did you do that? You just opened the garage door and we're hundreds of miles away! There are *tooooools* in the garage!" She said "tools" as if she was saying "gold bullion." "The lawnmower. Your father's snow blower. Those nice lawn chairs we got from Sears! Nick, turn around, we have to go back home!"

I reached forward, pushed the button again and said, "There, it's closed. We've trapped the burglar, call 911."

She wasn't convinced. For the rest of the vacation, the garage door was on her mind. Had we had cell phones back in those days, she could have called a neighbor and asked them to check on the door. Instead, she stewed, for an entire week until we returned home to see the garage door closed. As it slowly opened upon arrival, I could see her peering under the door, convinced the robber would still be in there. Perhaps parched and dehydrated now, from lack of nourishment.

I inherited anxiety from my mother. I was bald until I was five-years-old. I used to pull my hair out in my sleep. Today they call this Trichotillomania, which is a form of obsessive-compulsive disorder in which patients feel the urge to pull or twist their hair until it breaks off. In those days, doctors simply attributed it to stress. I was under too much stress, said my doctor. I was five. What the heck does a five-year-old have to be under too much stress about? "Oh my goodness, I've got a big game of Operation in the morning and I didn't get my nap in today. My Big Wheel's making this clicking sound when I pedal and I don't have the cash to get it fixed right now. My Easy Bake Oven is on the fritz, now how will I make that soufflé?" Rip. Rip. Rip. Rip.

Anxiety is in the Goich family genes.

It's no surprise that one of our favorite family pastimes is taking our blood pressure together. During this fourteen-day period, we'd have plenty of chances to do so. This afternoon as we took my mother's blood pressure, we all joined in and took ours, too. After my mom's stats were gathered, we all circled around the kitchen table and strapped on our monitors. 120/80 to us was the equivalent of an 810 FICO score to others. Some families gather together over a Scrabble board. Others play Trivial Pursuit. My family's activity of choice? The showdown between systolic and diastolic. We have turned blood pressure taking into a sport. The continual goal of having the lowest blood pressure is epic in our family. We each have our own personal "cuffs." I carry mine in my purse. My parents keep theirs on their kitchen table, taking their blood pressure every morning when they wake up, and each night when they go to bed. My dad travels with his and marks his numbers in his journal every morning. My sister keeps hers at her bedside. When people visit, we offer to take their blood pressure, too. Why not share the fun? If we had the proper equipment, I think we'd probably do urine samples, too. I don't like to think we're hypochondriacs so much as we're frustrated physician wannabees.

At the end of day four, my mom's blood pressure was perfect. In fact, she won the competition that day. It didn't look like she'd be going anywhere any time soon. Though we could see subtle changes in her physical body, her insides seemed to be chugging along just fine. When would the tide turn?

Day 5

"Don we now our gay apparel . . ."

"Be good to Teddy," my mom said as we sat watching *The View* like it was any other normal morning during any other normal visit over any other normal year I've sat in this same spot with her.

Teddy is my husband, a catch my mom was so thrilled I finally made. Not marrying until my late thirties, she feared I would never find someone to take care of me. She hated to think I was drifting alone, 3,000 miles away, further than her apron strings would reach.

"I will, Mother. As long as he's good to me."

She squeezed my hand.

On this 349th day of 2011, our morning chores and cleanup were finished and we were having a moment of togetherness while my sister was on the phone in the back bedroom.

"Don't fight with him," she continued.

"But you and Father fought my entire life. And you turned out okay."

"Love is better if you don't fight at all."

My mom taught me about love. She taught me about generosity. She taught me to respect my elders, my teachers, my friends and those less fortunate. She taught me to lead with my heart, treat people the way that I would want to be treated, and to never bully or tease. She taught me to walk, to put sponge rollers in my hair and how to shine my patent leather shoes with Vaseline for church on Sundays.

But the one thing my mom never taught me about was boys. I don't know why, but I never learned the boy basics. It was Debbie Brewington who gave me "the sex talk," behind the garage in her backyard when I was seven. My mom never once mentioned it to me. I learned about my period in hygiene class (Do schools even have hygiene class anymore?). Had my mom just once sat me down and said, "Lisa, if you want a boy, sit back and let him come to you," my life would have been totally different. I might have married Billy Pepper and had three kids by the time I was twenty-two.

Ahhhh . . . Billy Pepper. From an early age, I was a boy chaser. Poor Billy Pepper was my first victim circa grade four. He had red curly hair and a mole on his cheek. I thought he was the cutest thing I had ever laid my eyes on. He was a tap dancer (that should have been my first clue). I did everything in my power to get Billy Pepper's attention. I'd sit next to him, draw pictures of him in art class, gaze at him longingly from across the crowded classroom, let him hit me with the ball in gym class during dodge ball. He never once looked my way. But that didn't stop me. I had zero concept of "hard to get." My motto was "if at first you don't succeed, mow him over with a tractor."

We would have square dancing on Friday in gym class. One week—rather than have our teacher pair us up—the teacher let girls pick boys. "Oh man, this is my chance!" I said with glee! I pushed my way to the front of the line so that no one else would get their hands on my hot little ginger before I could. When Mrs. McMillan called my name, I could hear the angels sing. In slow motion, I walked toward Billy Pepper, reached out my hand as we were formally taught to do when offering a dance to someone in square dancing and Billy looked at my hand, turned on his toes and do-si-do'd right out of there. In front of the whole class, I was rejected by Billy Pepper. It was the first of many humiliations I'd receive in my lifetime at the hands of a boy. Unfortunately, not the last from Billy.

Yes, I went back for more. (See: "If at first I don't succeed . . ." above).

It was the end of the year in fourth grade. Autograph books were popular at the time. The little rectangular books with their pages folded into triangular origami shapes were our Twitter, our Facebook and our Instagram rolled into one. I handed my book to Billy Pepper and asked him to sign it. He asked if he could bring it home and give it back to me the next day. *Are you kidding me*? You mean, my autograph book would travel back to Billy Pepper's *house* with him tonight? Sit on his dining room table? Maybe be opened on the floor in front of his TV? Perhaps he'd take it to . . . I can't even go there . . . *bed* with him and tuck it under his pillow as he fell asleep? Oh, this was just too much for me to handle.

"Um . . . yeah!" I said. "Just bring it back to school tomorrow." I skipped away with love in my eyes and hearts rolling down my sleeves.

This is a feeling I would replicate over and over and over again during my lifetime. Letting a boy's actions determine my level of happiness.

I could hardly sleep that night. Sugar plum, unicorned, white and pink glitter dreams filled my head. I laid there on my back, staring at my

Bobby Sherman and David Cassidy posters on the wall, certain that Billy Pepper was laying on his back thinking of me and thinking about the message of love he was going to pen to me. Perhaps he'd write my name, "Lisa" with a heart above the i. Or he'd put the interlocking TLA at the bottom of the page for "True Love Always." Or he'd put his school picture inside the book, with a secret message written to me on the back. The anticipation was so sweet. I never wanted the wondering to end.

The following day, we were sitting in the auditorium. Billy Pepper was in the row behind me. He tapped me on the shoulder and passed my autograph book to me. I didn't want to read it in front of him so I tucked it in my school bag and brought it home to read that night. After dinner that evening, I prepared for the unveiling ceremony by going into my bedroom, closing the door, putting on some music—The Partridge Family, of course—sitting on my bed and pulling the autograph book out of my school bag.

While David Cassidy crooned "I Think I Love You," I held my future in my hands. I opened the autograph book to the last folded page and flipped the fold back to reveal Billy's handwriting. The first thing I saw was a little stick figure of a guy smoking a cigarette. So dreamy. Then I read the message. "To a stupid kid with no sense. Ha ha ha. Billy Pepper." Now I know why they call it a crush. That's exactly what it did to me. I felt a giant fist come down from the sky and pound itself on the top of my head, driving my body into my mattress, splattering my heart all over my yellow flowered bedspread. And it wasn't until forty years later—when I saw his name listed as a member of the *Gay Men's Chorus of Los Angeles*—that I finally gained my closure.

For all I know, my mom never went through anything similar to this. She never experienced heartache at the hands of a boy. At least not that I knew of. Maybe that's why she never talked to me about it. She was married to my dad at twenty-one and stuck by his side for over six decades. I don't think she was ever dumped in her life. I wish, now, I would have asked her in those last days. I wish I knew more about my mom and her life. I wish I knew if she ever loved someone deeply in her lifetime that wasn't my dad. Or was my dad her first and only? How is it possible that I came from my mom's womb yet was so different from her in this regard? I had a crush every minute from elementary through college. If I wasn't in love, it wasn't a day worth living. My self-worth was firmly attached to the boys in my life I loved at any particular moment. Why didn't my mom stop this from happening? Why did my mom let me do this? She may as well have watched me fall headfirst into heroin addiction, because that's how difficult it was to pry me away from some of these bozos. Maybe she just didn't know any better because she hadn't been through it herself. Or maybe she had and just wanted me to learn my own lessons the hard way.

A car horn honked in the driveway and the sound of the electric garage door rolling on its tracks followed. My brother, Richard, and sister-in-law, Kathy, arrived with my niece, Sara, her daughter, Emme, and their dog, Mimi, in tow. At just two months old, Emme, my parents' first great grandchild, brought a lot of joy to my mom during this time. Though Emme was far too young to comprehend what was going on—and she will never remember any of it when she's older or have any recollection of her great grandmother—she was an integral part of the process and it was good for my mom's soul to have her with us for those two weeks.

"Mother, Emme's here!" I said, motioning Sara to come to my mom's bed so she could see her new great granddaughter.

"Emme. Oh she's so beautiful. Come here to Baba, Emme." My mom raised her arms from her bed, in an attempt to hold the baby.

My niece Sara slipped Emme's coat off and rested her on top of my mom's chest so my mom could get a closer look.

"You're going to be a heartbreaker one day, my sweet baby," my mom said, Emme gripping her finger and almost dwarfing my mom who seemed particularly small even with a newborn laid across her bed.

Emme took it all in, never crying, just letting my mom love her. A relationship that would last only nine more days. This was the only Emme my mom would ever know.

I thought back to a trip we all took to her beloved Las Vegas the year before. Her last vacation. Though she was quite frail, she wanted to visit Sin City "one more time" while my niece Sara was living and working at a hospital there. I flew in from Los Angeles to join them and we had a truly memorable weekend together. My mom tore through the casinos with her walker like her legs were battery-operated. She pulled the handles of the slot machines with abandon, her fingers black from nickel stains, my niece's partner Eric by her side, reading her the displays she couldn't see through her haze-covered eyes.

"You got two cherries and a bar, Millie. Try again!" Eric would say.

And my mom would put three more tokens in the slot machine, pull the handle and ask, "Did I get anything good?"

This went on all day. We ate, and gambled, ate and gambled. You would hardly know that my mom's painful scoliosis existed or that she couldn't see two feet in front of her. Las Vegas injected her with a magical serum that made every one of her ailments disappear.

After dinner the first night, we all retreated back to Sara and Eric's for news they wanted to share with my parents in person. I had made a booklet with a series of 8.5 x 11 color photographs to present to my mom and dad. Sara handed my mom the book, who started thumbing through the pictures. Not sure, at first what she was looking at, she glanced quizzically at Sara and Eric asking, "What is this?"

"What do you think it is?" asked Eric.

My dad squinted his eyes, not able to make out the photographs and my mom turned the book upside down hoping that would offer a better clue.

"It's your great granddaughter, Baba," Sara replied. "In my belly."

"My great granddaughter? Whose . . . what . . ." then it hit her. "Well I'll be goddamn," said my mom (in a good way) then started to cry.

"We're having a baby!" I said enthusiastically. Not getting a clear read on their reaction, I asked, "Are you guys okay with this?" I wasn't sure how they would feel about the fact that Sara and Eric weren't married and were having a child. Would this factor into their opinion at all? Would an eighty-four-year-old and eighty-eight-year-old judge them for not abiding by the "first comes love, then comes marriage, then comes baby in the baby carriage," rule?

"Why wouldn't we be okay with this?" asked my mom. "I'm going to be a great grandmother!"

My parents were so hip.

With that, my mom said, "Let's go back to the casino!" and grabbed her purse. It was time to celebrate with more nickels and cherries and bells and bars.

And today, as she held little Emme close to her chest, I thought about how exhausted she made me that weekend in Vegas. How I begged her to slow down and maybe save some gambling for the following day. How all I wanted to do was go back to my niece's house and rest for awhile. What I wouldn't do to follow her around a casino just one more time, trailing behind her with her giant cup of coins jingling in her hands.

My sister-in-law brought lunch for all of us and, after we ate, the three siblings—me, my brother and sister—sat at the kitchen table and signed forms making us the beneficiaries of my parents' various accounts and policies. Signing paperwork seemed so cold and official during this otherwise warm and fuzzy process. It was much easier to pretend my mom was going to live forever if we didn't have to face realities like insurance policies and wills. It was all very grown up and I didn't quite feel like being a grown up right now.

My mom summoned us all into the family room for an announcement.

"I know what I want to wear in my casket!" she said, her eyes bright like she was about to tell us about a new outfit she bought for a wedding. "Lisa, go get the bag in my bedroom."

I went into my parents' bedroom and pulled out the bag my cousin and his wife had delivered the day before.

"Open it!" my mom instructed.

I reached into the bag and pulled out a white sweatshirt. I unfolded the shirt and turned it toward my brother and sister-in-law with a "Ta Da!" motion of my wrists.

"Thank you for coming?" my brother read, with a tone of confusion in his voice.

"Yeah!" my mom said. "Thank you for coming! To my funeral! Isn't it funny?!"

I let out a huge "Ha!" Perfect, I thought. The most genuine expression of my mother's personality and gratitude.

"I think it's totally you, Mother," I said, smiling. "And it'll be warm."

"Isn't it funny? I want to be funny. And look, it has an Ohio State logo underneath it with a U of M logo next to that to honor the two favorite men in my life: my husband and my son."

I couldn't have been more in support of this idea. "Brilliant!" I said. It was so my mom that, in my opinion, it was case closed.

But not everyone saw humor in the sweatshirt.

"Shouldn't she wear a *dress*?" Richard asked.

"Definitely a dress," Kathy chimed in, echoing my brother's sentiments.

"I will *not* have my mother wear a silly sweatshirt in her casket!" my brother said firmly.

"That's ridiculous," Kathy reaffirmed.

"It's not our decision to make, guys. If she wants to wear this sweatshirt, let her wear this sweatshirt. What's the big deal?"

"I will not have her make a clown of herself. She's wearing a dress," exclaimed my brother. "End of discussion."

I walked out of the room without responding, retreated to my bedroom and closed my door. Tensions were running high as it was at this time, and I felt we didn't need more family friction to make things worse. My mom spent most of her life at the mercy of other's decisions so this shouldn't have been a surprise. My mom thought of this idea on her own, inspired by a story told to her by a nurse in the hospital. It was a final expression of her creativity that she wanted to execute. She had a light in her eyes I hadn't seen the entire time I had been home when I pulled the shirt out of the bag. She was *excited*. I was seething at this point. I turned off the lights, got under my covers and slept. I didn't come out of my room until my brother left for the evening and the coast was clear.

I walked out into the family room. My sister was sitting at my mom's bedside talking to her. My mom saw me come into the room and asked me where I had been.

"Sleeping, Mother. I'm not feeling too well." A ridiculous statement, considering I was talking to a dying woman.

I wanted to tell her I was angry with my brother and sister-in-law about their protestation over the sweatshirt. But I didn't want to upset her. So I gently brought the subject up and simply asked her, "Mother, how much does it mean to you to wear that sweatshirt after you go?"

"Oh, I think it will be so funny! Don't you think people will like it?"

"I think people will love it, Mother. And I think it's something they'd expect from you. And it's something that will make them smile when they see you, and later down the line when they think back on you wearing it."

"I do too," said my mother.

"But Richard and Kathy aren't on board with the sweatshirt. They want you to wear a dress. Would you be opposed to wearing a dress?"

My mom didn't respond. I could see the bubble bursting in her heart. I could see her need to please rising to the surface, never wanting anyone to be angry or in opposition with her. She looked defeated.

My dad was sitting silent in his chair, listening, but purposely keeping himself out of the conversation.

My sister wasn't commenting on the sweatshirt, but I know she would have been on the side of whatever my mom wanted. After all, it was my mom's life—no one else's. If she wanted to wear a ballet tutu, she should have been able to. It wasn't our call to make.

I decided to let the subject lie for the night until we all had a chance to sleep on it. We'd revisit it in the morning. My brother would be back the next day and we could all discuss it as a family. Maybe they'd come around.

Day 6

"I love Thee, Lord Jesus; look down from the sky
And stay by my cradle 'til morning is nigh . . ."

The morning never seemed so quiet at my parents' house. I strained to hear the compressor pumping air into the mattress on my mom's hospital bed in the family room. "Ker Phhhhh-hhhh, Ker Phhhhhhh," as it drew air in and out of the mattress, keeping my mom's blood circulating evenly through her body. My mom had a rough night the evening before, waking up at 2 a.m. after soiling herself in her sleep. Not able to move from her bed, she was forced to defecate where she lay. And not wanting to wake anyone, she remained in that position until she finally couldn't take it any longer. She woke my dad who was sleeping next to her. My dad started the cleanup process, but overwhelmed, woke my sister and me up to help him clean my mom, remove her nightgown and change and wash her bedding. She was embarrassed and frustrated.

"I just want to die already! I can't live like this any longer!"

"Mother, we're here for you," I assured her. Don't be embarrassed and don't beat yourself up. This is why we're here. We love you. So stop talking like that."

As my mom lay naked from the waist down, I lifted up her legs like a toddler, while my sister slid a pad under her hips. I got a diaper out of the package left by the hospice nurse and placed it on my mom. Never having had children, this was foreign to me. But I had diapered plenty of baby dolls to know the general vicinity of where and how this thing should go on. This would be the way my mom would relieve herself from now until the end. No more potty. No more nighttime accidents. Self-contained bowel movements were much easier to deal with than unexpected explosions. I pulled her nightgown down over her hips and ran a baby wipe over her legs for a final cleanse.

"Just let me go to bed. Okay? Just let me go to bed." She turned her head away from us and I could see tears rolling down her cheek.

I pulled the covers over her, kissed her goodnight, and my sister took the soiled linens down into the basement to wash. Peeling off my rubber gloves, I discarded them in a plastic bag that I tied up and threw into a bin in the garage. I washed my hands then coated them with hand sanitizer, something I had been doing at least fifteen times a day since adopting the job of caregiver. We all went back to our rooms, my dad retiring back to the couch.

As I walked away, I could hear my mom weeping.

Five hours later, I awoke to the sound of the air mattress compressor on my mom's bed. After last night's episode, my dad was still asleep. He hadn't been waking up early since my mom had been back home and immobile. My mom had been my dad's alarm clock for sixty-four years. Without her to open the curtains in the morning, regardless of whether or not my dad was fast asleep, hindered his ability to know whether it was light outside or dark. So he continued to sleep. The unspoken rule in our house had always been that when my mom woke up, the whole house woke up. And without my mom to guide us now, we were lost.

I love sleeping in. Always have. Always will. For some reason, my mom had always been adamantly against me sleeping. I say she was against me sleeping because it's clear that she would be unhappy when I wasn't awake when she determined I should be. Through high school, I could hear her lie to people on the phone when I was sleeping in the morning and someone would call me. "Oh, Lisa's not here right now. Can I take a message?" I'd mumble under my breath from under my covers. I'd call her out on it, but she never had a concrete reason why she chose to tell a fib rather than just tell whoever was calling, "She's in bed. She got home late. She'll call you when she wakes up." I'd ask her why she lied and she'd say, "I'm not going to tell them you're *sleeping*." And she'd say the word "sleeping" like it was a dirty word. It would have been easier for her to say, "Lisa is out breaking into cars this morning" than it would have been for her to tell one of my friends that I was sleeping. This was utterly painful in the years following college when many nights I'd stumble in drunk at 3 a.m., with the smell of Brad Phillips on my lips and Michelob Lite in my belly. She never punished me coming in, but she'd get me on the other side of dreamland in the morning.

My mom's morning M.O. was always the same. She would get out of bed and immediately open the curtains in her bedroom. This did two things: made noise and flooded the room with light. I could still hear those curtains opening in my head. "Ksssssssh, Ksssssssh, Ksssssssssh," as she pulled the cord three times for each set of panels. She would then walk from her bedroom across the hall and swing my door open hard enough for the doorknob to hit the wall behind it. The light from her bedroom would pour into my room, summoning my eyes to open.

Shuffling further down the hallway, into the kitchen, she would turn on the transistor radio that sat atop their kitchen hutch since 1967, and crank the volume up to about 24 (the maximum volume on the radio is 25). She'd then step down into the family room and turn on the TV. Both mediums would be battling for entertainment supremacy; *Regis & Kathie Lee* screaming from the family room, while *Jim Harper & the Breakfast Club* tried to top the morning duo's feigned mutual admiration from the kitchen.

When I wouldn't respond to the open door, the light pouring in from the open curtains or the TV & Radio aural assault, she would up the ante by tossing some bacon in a pan. Now my olfactory senses were kicking in. She was hitting me from every one of my weak points until I couldn't bear it any longer.

"Okay, I'm up! You win!"

"I didn't tell you you had to wake up. Why don't you go back to bed?" she'd say in a slightly martyr-like tone.

But this morning, it was different. There was no noise. No curtains opening, no toilet flushing, no bacon in the pan. It was simply, "Ker Phhhhhhhhh, Ker Phhhhhhh," as the compressor shifted weight from my mom's left calf to her left thigh, then back down her legs to her right thigh then her right calf. I never thought I'd say this, but I missed my mom's clanking around. I wanted to hear those curtains opening again. I wanted the light to flood my room. I wanted my mom back.

So I stayed in bed, staring at the cat mobile on the ceiling from the Museum of Modern Art that had lived there since 1985, watching as the silhouettes of kitties jumped over balls and batted yarn as they spun around in circles. After an hour of feline acrobatics, my phone rang. I looked at the phone and saw Mitch Albom's name on the screen. Mitch was my friend and former colleague. In addition to his work as a *New York Times* bestselling author and award-winning newspaper columnist, Mitch hosted an afternoon drive talk radio show in Detroit. I worked on his radio show for many years as an on-air sidekick and producer. My parents adored Mitch. And Mitch loved my parents. I had emailed Mitch earlier in the week when I knew I'd be in town for at least two weeks, and to tell him about my mom's prognosis. I told him that it was a tough road and that we were doing the best we could to keep my mom comfortable.

"I'm so tired, Mitch," I confessed.

"How often do the hospice workers come to the house?" he asked.

"An aide comes once in the morning and once at night to help with hygienic care, and a nurse comes every other day. Otherwise, my sister and I are handling the bulk of the every day cleaning and tasks. It's difficult. Seeing my mom in this state is just so, so hard. And all of our patience is wearing thin. Ours. Hers. We're all spent."

As the author of the mega-bestselling memoir, *Tuesdays With Morrie*, Mitch knew this drill better than most. In fact, he had become a bit of a guru in the field of death and dying after his days spent with Morrie Schwartz, his beloved professor, who battled ALS. People—total strangers—turned to Mitch with questions about these final, mysterious days in their loved ones' lives. How blessed I was to have a private audience with him.

"How about hiring additional care to fill in the gaps when the hospice workers can't be there?" Mitch asked.

"They only offer the care morning and night."

"I'm not talking about hospice," he added. "I'm talking about a few more hands to help around the house."

"Well, that sure would be nice, but we can't afford it. And insurance won't pay for it."

"I have an idea. I'll call you back," Mitch said, then hung up the phone.

About fifteen minutes later, my cellphone rang. It was a local Detroit number I didn't recognize and I picked up.

"This is Lisa," I answered.

"This is Paul from Health Partners. Mitch Albom asked for me to call you. First, I'm very sorry to hear about your mother."

"Thank you, Paul. I appreciate it."

"I understand you might need some additional help around the house the next week or two."

"Well, as I told Mitch, we could certainly use the help, but can't really afford anything that insurance can't cover."

"Mitch is taking care of it. Just let me know what you need and how often you need it and we'll send someone over later today."

"Mitch is taking care of the whole thing?"

"Yep. Just let us know exactly what you need and we'll take care of the rest."

My sister had been up earlier, made some tea, and retreated back to her room to work on her computer. My mom was still asleep. I went out into the family room and checked on my mom. Yes, the blankets were moving. Yes, she was still alive.

I sat in my dad's chair and turned on the television. I had no idea what day it was at this point. The presence of *Good Morning America* indicated to me that it was a weekday. But beyond that, I had no idea if it was Monday or Thursday. In fact, it was Friday. The weekend was upon us, but that meant nothing to me. Our days were no longer determined by week or weekend, but by what number we were on. Knowing that my mom had approximately two weeks to live, we knew we were on Day 6 and we still had some quality time left to spend as a family. That's all that mattered. Weekends were for the other people out there. We were in here. And all that was important was my mom.

My mom opened her eyes and asked for some water. My dad was still asleep, with his eye shades on and the faux fur brown blanket pulled up over half his face. I grabbed my mom's blue plastic cup with the straw from the end table, filled it with some fresh water and lifted it to her mouth. I had to place the straw in her mouth and hold it there because her hands were unsteady. She spit the straw out and motioned the cup away, indicating she had had enough.

"What are you watching?" she asked. "Turn it up, I can't hear it."

"Morning shows, Mother. What do you want to watch?"

"This is good."

My mom has always loved knowing what was going on in the world. And she was very well-rounded in her knowledge. She could tell you box office numbers, who was dating whom, what world leader was in hot water this week and which stint in rehab Lindsay Lohan was on. Aside from the poor hearing and eyesight, she was sharp. *Good Morning America* ran a clip of an interview Ellen DeGeneres did with then thirteen-year-old Paris Jackson, daughter of Michael, which aired the day before. My mom watched as Jackson discussed a movie she was starring in and what it was like growing up as the daughter of the late pop legend.

"Those poor kids," my mother said. "Lived such a weird life, now without a father." I just realized the irony of my mom outliving Michael Jackson. Staring at my mother immobile in bed, it was a stark contrast to the vision of the moonwalking, gloved Jackson I had spinning around in my head.

"I like that Ellen, though," she added. "I think it's nice she's gay."

"I think it's nice, too." I smiled at my mom's innocence. And her openness. And thought to myself how thankful I was to have a mother like her.

"Why's it so loud in here?" my dad grumbled from the couch. "Jesus Christ, turn down that TV."

"Father, it's almost ten o'clock. Time to wake up."

He pulled the covers over his face, and my dog Angie jumped on him when she saw that he was awake. She loved my dad. All dogs love my dad. He was the Dog Whisperer before there ever was a Dog Whisperer.

As an adult, my first dog was a scruffy and sometimes grumpy terrier mix named Oliver. Oliver was my dad's kindred spirit. When we would fly from Los Angeles to Detroit—pre-9/11 in the days when people could still meet you at the gate—Oliver would spot my dad as we exited the plane and start scratching at the mesh on his dog carrier, eager to kiss my dad's face and have my dad lead him out of the airport. When Oliver died I had him cremated. His ashes remained at my parents' house and will eventually be placed in my dad's casket with him, at my dad's request.

My dad swung his legs over the side of the couch, squinted his eyes, and pet Angie as she sat in his lap.

"How'd you sleep, Mika?" he asked. Mika being my dad's pet name for my mom.

"Good after that shit episode last night. No more of that. I don't want any more of that."

My dad grabbed her hand and they both stared at the TV.

"I have some good news, you two!" I said, trying to divert the subject from last evening's nightmare.

No one responded.

"Mitch Albom called this morning. He sends his love and is going to come over to visit you later in the week."

"Oh, that's nice!" my mom said. "I like that Mitch."

"Then you're really going to like this. Mitch has offered to pay for your home health care from now until . . . until . . . until well, until you don't need it anymore." I couldn't get myself to say, "until you die."

My mom and dad both turned their eyes from the television toward each other. Then looked at me. Then looked back at each other.

"He's paying for everything?" my dad asked.

"Everything. Whatever we need over and above what hospice is offering us. So if you want someone here round-the-clock, he'll take care of it. He wants to take care of you. Just let me know what you want and he'll make it happen."

My mom began to cry. My dad wiped her eyes. I told her how much she was loved and we all sat for a while, thankful for the blessings and friends we had in our lives.

Ten minutes had passed. "I think I'm gonna wear the dress in my casket," exclaimed my mom out of the blue.

"The dress?" I asked.

"Yeah, a dress. I don't need to wear the sweatshirt. Maybe we can just fold the sweatshirt up and put it on a table somewhere. I don't want to cause any troubles. A dress will be nice."

Making peace while eliminating waves. My mother should have been a diplomat. She probably thought about that sweatshirt all night long.

"You know what dress looked nice on you? That blue dress you wore to that wedding. When I did your hair and put the blue eyeshadow on you? The one in the picture in the dining room."

"Oooooh, yeah!" said my mom excitedly. "That's a pretty dress. Go get it for me. Maybe we can put a sweater over it. And my jewelry. Get my jewelry."

Riding the wave of my mom's enthusiasm, my sister and I went into the bedroom, pulled the blue dress out of the closet and began assembling different versions of the outfit for my mom to take into consideration. And ultimately for my brother and sister-in-law to take into consideration, since they were the ones championing the dress idea. We found a beautiful hand crocheted white sweater with pretty Lucite buttons. In the photo she had been wearing clear beads and earrings. We located those in her jewelry box and laid them on top of the dress on the bed. It looked perfect.

We scanned the floor of her closet for an appropriate pair of shoes. Had she been in the room with us picking out her own footwear, my mom would have chosen her beloved gym shoes (she always called them "gym shoes," not tennis shoes). And though no one can see your feet in a casket, I was sure someone would have a problem with her wearing gym shoes for all of eternity, so I pulled out a pair of silver flats from the back of the closet and set them on the floor at the side of the bed just underneath the dress. Squinting and tilting my head, trying to picture this as an outfit on my mom as she laid in rest, I realized how surreal this was. I was picking out an outfit for my mom, not for an event, but for her death. Her funeral clothes. Her last hurrah.

In a perfect world, we would dress her in one of her beloved horizontal striped shirts and a pair of capris. Several pastel-striped shirt sleeves peeked out from between sweater sets in her closet. Next to each shirt was a pair of matching capris: baby blue, soft pink, light yellow. Her little pants were so tiny; in the last few years of her life she had to purchase them from the children's department so they would fit her seventy-pound frame. She liked her tops roomier to accommodate the hump she had developed from scoliosis. She never wanted to accentuate her back with tight fitting shirts, and would wear a medium or large so it would drape neatly over her deformed spine.

I walked to the closet and pulled one of these shirts out, bringing it to my nose, inhaling so I could let my mom's scent fill my soul. She had

had this shirt for years. Not just five years, but twenty years. At least. I had a framed picture of my mom sitting on a bench in Mexico holding a peso and smiling in her wide-brimmed sun hat wearing this shirt.

When I was in my late twenties, and flush with a little cash from my job as an advertising copywriter, I decided to take my mom on a vacation to Cancún. Just the girls. My mom and me. Of course Cancún was the logical choice of a holiday destination for a woman who hated the sun and never set foot on a beach. Not sure what my line of thinking was back then, but at the time it seemed like the perfect getaway. Two hot señoritas taking over the Yucatán Peninsula. While I baked in the sun every day, my mom kicked her feet up on a lounge chair underneath a cabana staring out at the Caribbean Sea, swatting away children peddling packages of Chiclets gum on the beach. Wearing her signature cataract sunglasses, and three-quarter inch sleeved striped shirts, she sipped fancy fruity drinks and—despite her aversion to beach life—I think actually enjoyed the relaxation she experienced not having to do anything for an entire week. A true luxury for a woman who spent her entire life making sure everyone else's needs were met around her and ignoring her own.

Where Danskin leggings were the personal style choice of Vera Wang, so were three-quarter inch sleeved striped shirts for Millie Goich. My mom never wore a tank top, spaghetti straps, halter or tube top in her life. Never a bathing suit in my forty-nine years of life with her. As a child, an accident involving her arm getting stuck in the wringer of a washing machine left her upper arm badly scarred. Embarrassed by this, she covered it up. Later in my life, I developed the same penchant for three-quarter inch sleeves. But in my case, it was to hide the perimenopausal arm flaps that started to develop in my late forties. Maybe my mom was on to something after all.

I hung the shirt back in my mom's closet and took a final look at the outfit laid out on the bed. Satisfied with our ensemble, my sister and I brought the clothes into the family room to show my parents. My mom loved the outfit. She was happy. My dad had a hard time looking at the dress and nodded only to appease my mom. Holding back his emotions, as we all were, he said, "You're gonna look pretty, Mika. Just like you always do."

Later that afternoon my brother and sister-in-law returned.

"I'm wearing a dress," my mom informed them. "Show Richard and Kathy the dress we picked out."

My sister and I led them into my parents' bedroom to show them what my mom had agreed on. Everyone was satisfied. My dad, for the first time that week, left my mom's side to go bowling. Something we had encouraged him to do to get his mind off the situation and also to get out with his friends and get some fresh air.

As another day wrapped up, I thanked God for this very special time we were all given to say goodbye to our matriarch. Wishing we could freeze time, I wasn't looking forward to Day 7, which—if all went as the doctors said it would—would be the halfway point between my mom's life, and death.

Day 7

"And heaven and nature sing, and heaven and nature sing . . ."

Waiting for someone to die isn't entirely unlike waiting for a cake to bake or clothes to dry or the cable guy to show up. You sit. You watch the clock. And wait. Everything needs to be put on hold because you don't know if it will happen today or tomorrow or next week or the week after that. Some days you don't feel like it's going to happen at all. Life gets put on hold because someone else's life is being extinguished.

As my mom lay in her hospice bed in the middle of the family room, we all watched the clock. Every day. She watched it, too.

"Am I still here?" she'd ask.

"Yes, Mother, you're still here."

"Shit," she'd respond.

And we'd all go back to watching TV. And watching the clock. My mom making phone calls to people she wanted to have final words with. Sharing goodbyes and I love yous. And the rest of us saying "shit" ourselves because we didn't know when "it" would happen. And our lives remained on hold.

I felt guilty for thinking about the things I had to do other than being with my dying mother. With idle time on your hands, it's easy to have thoughts wander in and out. To-do lists remaining unchecked. Errands not being run. When someone dies: Time. Stands. Still.

Christmas was one of those things on my mind. In forty-nine years, I had never not celebrated Christmas. The parties I was missing, the decorations I would never put up, the popcorn that wouldn't be strung this year. (Okay, so I had never actually strung popcorn in my life, but the vision of doing so helped me to feel even more sorry for myself than I already did. And that felt good to me at the time.)

None of it really mattered to me, but at the same time, it did. I kept counting the days, saying, "If my mom died today, and we had a funeral, would I get home in time to put up Christmas lights?" Then I'd beat myself up wondering what kind of a daughter I was to think of something like that.

And then there were the Bob Seger tickets. I felt extreme guilt for not giving up a pair of tickets I purchased for a show at the Staples Center in Los Angeles. I couldn't bring myself to return them, just in case. Just in case she'd go a couple days shy of the show. They were really good seats; great seats, in fact. The most money I had ever paid for concert tickets in my life. One of the perks of being married to a musician is that you get into just about every concert for free. With VIP passes, backstage access and after parties. But my tickets to Bob Seger were just as a mere civilian. A fan from Detroit who was looking forward, more than anything, to seeing this show 2,294 miles from the family room I was currently sitting in.

The concert was December 27th. Ten days away. My mom's blood pressure was still perfect, her heart was still beating, her spirits were still high. She didn't look like she'd be going anywhere anytime soon. "When is she going to die?" became the question we'd all ask ourselves, the nurses, and each other every day. We wouldn't quite be so blunt, it was more of a, "So is she . . . you know . . . how is her . . . what can we expect in the next few days?" sort of inquiry. One part of me was hoping the process would speed up so that I could go on with my life and go to this show. Ashamed to admit it, I'd had enough of diapering and poop wiping and tooth brushing and hair combing and body flipping and care giving. I wanted to end the grieving. I wanted life to be normal again. I wanted to turn the page and let Bob Seger roll me away. But in reality, it was all a distraction to shift my focus from the inevitable. I knew I'd never use those tickets. But picturing myself anywhere other than where I was at the moment was like a warm blanket swaddling my broken soul.

❄

On the afternoon of Day 7, after returning from a much-needed hour and a half massage from my friend Cecilia, my niece Nicole and I were sitting with my mom in the family room. My dad was at the kitchen table paying bills and my sister was in the back guest bedroom meditating. She's from San Francisco. That's what people from San Francisco do. My mom was happy and still very coherent. We had so many guests in and out of the house up until this point, it was nice to have some quiet time with my mom. The hospice nurses had come and gone that morning. The first of Mitch's helpers stopped by after hospice left to give my mom some tender loving care. Her hair was washed, her teeth were brushed, her diaper was changed and her bedding was freshened. This was like a four-star resort for the dying. She wasn't eating anymore, other than an occasional lick or two of the giant lollipop my niece brought her earlier in the week. We'd try to give her food, but she refused. I wasn't sure if she just wasn't hungry, or if she was trying to speed up the dying process through starvation. Either way, she'd turn her head like a two-year-old when we'd put a fork near her lips. After seven days of this, we gave up trying.

It was an overcast day, wet and sleeting. The curtains to the back patio door were open, allowing my mom to see a little bit of the outdoors from her bed. Though she didn't venture into her backyard much—if at all—she always liked to see outside to report on the weather. "Oh God, it's gonna rain today." "Look at how dark that sky is!" "Turn the air on, Nick, it's gonna be a hot one!"

From as early as I can remember, my mom and dad have been obsessed with the weather. Which is ironic, seeing that she rarely experienced the weather from any place other than her sofa. She never even opened the windows in her house. In the summer they were closed while the air conditioner was on; in the winter they were closed, because of the bitter Michigan cold. Occasionally, she would allow some air in from the screened back patio door. But this wasn't very often. It usually only opened if there was a smoke alarm crisis from something burning in the kitchen, or there was a house full of people and we simply needed air.

An outdoorswoman Millie Goich was not.

We used to spend our summer nights on the back patio. It wasn't that large, but it was roomy enough to house a three-piece patio set, a dining table and chairs and a gas barbecue grill. I loved eating corn-on-the cob on that back patio on warm, Michigan summer nights. This all stopped a few years earlier when their awning over the back patio ripped. Rather than fix or replace it, my mom decided to keep it down. From that point forward, they never put their furniture back outside in the summers. And we never had another outdoor barbecue. If my dad wanted to sit in the yard—which he loved to do—he'd have to get a folding chair, set it up in the middle of the empty concrete slab, and make himself at home for a few hours with a good book under the sun.

Unlike my dad, my mom never ventured outside. Occasionally, she'd open the back patio door to "Psssssssttt" away a squirrel. She hated squirrels. I don't know where this animosity toward the fuzzy-tailed rodents started—it could have had something to do with the hamster I brought home one weekend from elementary school science class that got loose in the house, rendering my mom a hysterical mess—but if she'd see a squirrel in the yard, she'd push open the patio door, stand behind the screen and let out her warning call, "Psssssssssssssttttttttt! Psssssssssssstttttttt!" The squirrels would scamper out of the yard, over the fence and up a tree. My mom always looked pleased with her ac-complishment. She'd go back to the couch, pick up her handheld slot machine game, and continue playing until the next squirrel dared to set foot on her patio.

But on this grey afternoon, there were no squirrels outside. And if there were, my mom had little energy to "Pssssssstttt!" them away. Sit-ting on a stool at my mom's bedside, we talked about life and family and the peace my mom wished for her family's future. Nicole glanced outside and saw my mom and dad's neighbor, Kitty Finazzo, peering out of her bathroom window.

"Baba, look, Kitty Finazzo's looking at you," Nicole informed my mom.

When Kitty saw my niece looking toward her, the curtain swung shut. This wasn't an easy task for Kitty, since her window was over the bath tub. To look out the window, at all of 5'1", she would have had to stand on something to reach it. It was clear that Kitty really wanted to see what was going on in my parents' house.

Since my mom had been home from the hospital, she had not seen Kitty Finazzo. Kitty Finazzo had not seen my mom. Unbeknownst to Kitty Finazzo, she was on my mom's shit list. Getting on "The Shit List" wasn't a place you wanted to be. Because once you were on, it was really,

really difficult to get off. This isn't a list she pulled out very often. In fact, over the years, I recall only four people being on this list. For various reasons my mom would get ticked off and say, "I'm not talking to her again. She can go to hell." And that was it. You were officially on the list. Three of the people made it off the list, but it took years. And now, at the end of my mom's life, one person remained: Poor Kitty Finazzo.

What Kitty Finazzo did to get on the list wasn't shit-list-worthy in my opinion, but this was my mom's list, not mine, so I had to respect that. In a nutshell, Kitty Finazzo wouldn't let my parents temporarily park their car in her garage. That was it. And it wasn't even her decision, it was her son's. It happened three weeks earlier. This pissed my mom off exponentially.

"For all we have done for her over the years! We take her to the grocery store, drive her to the fruit market! And she won't let us park in her goddamned garage! To hell with her!" And that was it. Shit listed forever.

And that afternoon as Kitty peered into my mom's family room, I tried to urge my mom to change her mind.

"Let's call Kitty and have her come over. You've been friends for so long, it's only fair you give her the chance to say goodbye."

"She can go to hell," snapped my mother. Nicole and I looked at each other and laughed.

"But Mother, it wasn't even her decision. It was her son's."

"Lisa, I said no. Call her and tell her I said to . . . Go. To. Hell."

"Okay, I'll get right on that." Nicole and I traded glances, knowing that when my mom put her mind to something, there was no changing it. So we closed the curtains and turned on the TV and put our arms around my mom as she fell asleep. Apparently, wiping one's slate clean before he or she dies isn't always a priority.

❋

After a short nap, my mom woke up and said, "You know what I feel like? Polenta!" We all looked at each other, wide-eyed and shocked. This was the first time my mom had spoken of, or even cared about food, in a week. She must have had a dream that set the craving in motion.

Polenta is the Italian word for a porridge made from cornmeal, water, butter and salt. Historically it was served as a peasant dish in parts of Europe and was popular in America during the depression. "Cornmeal mush" as my mom called it when I was a kid, polenta sounded so much more appetizing and high society. We all loved my mom's polenta.

Definitely a comfort food, she would load it with butter and cheese and we'd make a meal out of it. Sometimes she would serve it as a side dish to pork chops, but many times we would just eat bowls of it for dinner. And sometimes I'd even eat it straight out of the pan.

Coincidentally, I had purchased some pre-made polenta in a roll when I had gone grocery shopping a couple of days before. I told my mom that I was going to make her "my recipe," and set out into the kitchen to do my magic. A cook, I was not. My sister, on the other hand, was a gourmet chef. Not by trade, but as a very serious hobby. So when I took out the scissors to clip off the end of the plastic wrap covering the polenta, then squeezed the roll onto a plate, I felt less like a culinary expert and more like a bachelor as I prepared our late afternoon snack. I cut the polenta into half-inch circles and placed them in a frying pan coated in olive oil. Frying both sides of the circles to a crisp, I sprinkled some cheddar cheese on the tops until it melted. I scooped two circles out of the pan and put them on a plate for my mom. And followed with two circles for my dad. Sprinkling on a little salt, then dabbing them each with a teaspoon full of sour cream, I brought my creation to my mom's bedside. I delivered my dad's to him at the kitchen table. My niece scooped off a small piece onto a spoon for my mom and fed it to her, as my mom fed my niece when she was a baby. "Mmmmmmm," said my mom. "This is good. You did a good job, honey."

My dad wasn't quite as complimentary.

"Do you like it, Father?"

"It's different," said my dad, chewing it like it was a chicken gizzard or pig's hoof or something that maybe he shouldn't be eating. "I like your mother's better," he continued.

"We all do, Father. But for now, this is what you're going to have to eat."

And then it hit me. I would never, ever eat my mom's polenta again. Neither would my dad. We wouldn't eat her polenta or palačinka or strudel or *Birdie In The Nest*. The thought made a thud in my stomach as I swallowed my tears. My mom would never cook for me again. I was on my own. I felt orphaned and lost at the realization that, "Oh my God, she really isn't going to be here anymore." It was easy to sweep that fact under the rug with all of the company and laughter and food and celebrating that had taken place the past week. And even though I knew what the end result of all of this merriment was, I didn't *know* what the end result was. Until now. Holy crap, my mother was going to die. What the heck was I going to do without her?

Day 8

DECEMBER 18

"Jolly Old Saint Nicholas, lean your ear this way;
Don't you tell a single soul what I'm going to say . . ."

"Are you ever going to get out of your pajamas?" my mom asked me as I sat next to her, folding sheets that had just come out of the dryer.

For the first time in six days I realized that, indeed, I was still in my pajamas. I hadn't showered, washed my hair, changed my clothes or put on even the minimum of makeup over the past week. I'm not sure if I brushed my teeth. I didn't even realize there was a 'me' to dress. My mind was solely on my mom. When I left the house for my massage, I wore my pajamas. My pajamas were comfortable, frankly. What was the point of getting dressed? And who was my mom to talk? She was in her pajamas, too. It was a two-week long pajama party and I, for one, wasn't ready to give up the attire.

This was Sunday. And Sunday meant football in the Goich house. My family, like most families in Detroit, is sports-minded through and through. They love their Lions (all sports teams in Detroit are spoken of in the possessive form, by the way), their Tigers, their Pistons, their Red Wings and their college teams. Though only my niece, Sara, graduated from the University of Michigan, U of M pride runs deep in our house. My dad, a Steubenville, Ohio native (home of Dean Martin!) always sides with the Buckeyes of Ohio State causing quite the family rivalry.

Today the Detroit Lions were playing the Oakland Raiders and my mom served as the centerpiece/cheerleader in the room while the entire immediate family screamed at the TV all around her. Everyone was present and my mom's space was filled with love. This was just like any other Sunday in my parents' family room, except for the fact that my mom was literally lying on her deathbed. It would probably be the last football game she'd ever watch—not that she cared. She—like me— couldn't care less about sports. I was my mom's clone and we preferred the sport of shopping over athletic competition any day.

As I snacked on potato chips and Faygo, my mom looked over at me and said, once again, "Why don't you go put some clothes on."

"Mother, I don't have any other clothes here to wear that are comfortable."

"You can't stay in your pajamas all day every day. Go get dressed. Make yourself look nice."

"I have nothing to wear," I repeated, a little more brusque this time.

"Then go buy something. Get out of the house. Go."

I must really look bad if a near-dead person is insisting I change my clothes, I thought to myself. On the other hand, perhaps she was just wanting me to breathe some air that wasn't recirculated from the oxygen machine feeding her lungs for the past seven days.

"Maybe I'll go to Target. Kristina can come with me."

"That's my girl," she said with a smile, tapping my hand gently with hers. "Kristina, take your sister to the store."

"Do you want me to get you anything while I'm there?" A question I have asked my mom a thousand times over the years, and today, realized the irony in it. What could my mom have wanted from Target, on this, the sixth day before her last day on Earth? A sweater? She wouldn't be needing it. Socks? Nope. A new purse? She won't be needing a purse where she's going.

"Want me to bring you home an Icee from the Target cafeteria?"

"Sure, that sounds good. Get me an Icee."

"What flavor?"

"Cherry."

"Deal." This request was encouraging seeing that my mom hadn't eaten in days, and was barely sipping from her blue plastic glass of water with the straw in it. At least the sugar could give her a little caloric boost and the drink would be refreshing.

I opted not to shower. Why ruin a good thing? Instead, I splashed some water on my face, tied my hair back in a ponytail, threw on a hat, a pair of jeans and my boots. My sister and I put on our coats, I grabbed the keys to my dad's Jeep and we said goodbye to the rest of the family who really weren't paying attention to our exit, but instead, were engrossed in the very close game unfolding on the TV. A light snow had fallen overnight and the driveway was dusted in white. Not enough for me to be reluctant to drive, but just enough to remind me that it was winter in Michigan. As we pulled out of the driveway, both of us let out a sigh of relief to be out of the house for a while. Neither of us had ventured out into civilization in days. And the cold air energized us as we headed on our journey.

"It's pretty heavy in there, isn't it?" I said to my sister.

"It's sad. But she's doing the right thing."

"I know. I know."

A familiar comfort came over me when we pulled into the Target parking lot. I was suddenly calm and happy. The bullseye was calling my name. I love Target. When I'm bored or down, I head to Target just to walk around, people watch, and buy more Mossimo t-shirts I really don't need. It's my happy place. Perhaps my mom was right. Maybe I did need to get something new to wear to perk me up and lift my spirits. At the very least, something new wouldn't smell. And though I couldn't smell myself, I'm assuming I wasn't the most pleasant person to be around that week.

Whenever I was in town, my mom and I would go to Target together. I would drive and she would push the cart, which served a double purpose: a receptacle for our day's haul and giant walker on wheels, steadying my mom as she strolled the aisles. My mom was fun to shop with. She was of the "if you like it, buy it," mentality. Not much for teaching me fiscal responsibility, but we sure did have a great time building our wardrobes.

Going to Target without my mom this day was another one of those light bulb moments that I'd have during this fourteen-day period. Not only was she not with me now, but she wouldn't be with me here again.

Ever. And as the Christmas carols filled the store and I passed horizontal striped sweaters, I was tempted to pick one up and toss it in the basket for her. At the same time, I realized that she would never be out of her pajamas again. Clothing—other than her funeral dress—would no longer be an option.

"Funeral dress! I have nothing to wear to the funeral!" I said to my sister, as we passed racks of skirts and blouses. I never thought about what I was going to wear to my mom's funeral. It seemed so far off, if it was going to happen at all. My mom's health—though not perfect— didn't seem to be declining to the point of a possible funeral. However, the nurses knew otherwise and continued to tell us that in about seven days she would be gone. How could that be? She wanted an Icee. People just don't die when they're still well enough to request an Icee.

Just then, a coat caught my eye. I didn't bring a warm coat with me from L.A. I always wore my mom's coats when I came to Detroit in the winter, rather than lug anything heavy with me on the plane. But the celadon green coat with the faux fur collar was dressy enough to be appropriate for a funeral, yet not too heavy to wear back in L.A. on a brisk California winter night. Plus buying it would make me feel good. And I really needed to feel good at that moment. There was one coat left on the rack—a medium—my size. Without even trying it on,

I tossed it in my basket and could hear my mom saying, "If you like it, buy it." So I did.

As I continued on my quest, nothing in the store seemed funeral-worthy. I had a navy blue dress at home that would be perfect. I'd have my husband bring it with him when he came. I bought a pair of tights to go with the dress. I found a pair of black pants and a blouse to wear to the funeral home the night before. I was set for the end. But I still needed something to hold me over for the next week. Something comfortable to live in, yet appropriate enough to receive guests. I settled on a pair of red and white flannel pants, dotted with snowflakes, with a long-sleeved red thermal shirt. And I couldn't pass up the red knee-high cable-knit slippers with the giant red ball ties on the sides. I knew my mom would like these, too, and thought about buying a pair for her. But I stopped myself. This was as close as I'd get to donning all our gay apparel this holiday season.

As we passed the jewelry section I thought that, perhaps, I should buy her a ring or a bracelet or something that she could wear with her funeral dress. But is that really how you want to send someone off? With a ring from Target? I think anything you wear for all of eternity should be meaningful in some way. Old, new, borrowed, blue. Or at the very least, expensive. Or handmade. So, instead, I decided to pick up a card that I would tuck into my mom's casket, written but not read, for her to open when she arrived at her final destination. We would put it in her pouch.

My mom's pouch was a purse I had made for her a year earlier to attach to the front of her walker. After her scoliosis had gotten to a critical point, she had a very hard time walking without assistance. Her walker had a seat attached to it that enabled her to sit when she was tired. She loved her walker. And she was hell on wheels when she strolled through the aisles of the grocery store, with a "Get out of my way, I'm coming through!" look on her face. I purchased the canvas for the pouch from a craft's store, along with the letters M-I-L-L-I-E in bright blue, to iron on the front pockets. I flanked her name with two red stars, which made the pouch Liberace fabulous. She used it when she went shopping, placing her credit card, her money and her coupons neatly in the pockets. When she would go to the casino with my dad, she'd put her player's card in the pouch, which entitled her to special casino perks. She loved the pouch.

We decided that the pouch was too nice to leave behind. So she requested to have it put into her casket. We had an idea to fill the pouch with goodbye offerings for my mom to take with her on her final trip. We encouraged people who visited to bring something for my mom to put inside—a picture, a note, a trinket—whatever it was they wanted my mom to remember them by. I added pictures of us together, some casino tokens, a few knick-knacks and would now add this card. I placed the card in the basket and headed to the check-out.

As my sister and I wrapped up our shopping, we were surrounded at the cash registers by parents with baskets overloaded with toys that would soon be wrapped and lovingly placed under Christmas trees. We didn't put a tree up this year. We didn't have any gifts to wrap. We had a basket full of funeral clothes. Santa would not be visiting Newport Drive this Christmas and we were fine with that. Our gift was these last few days with our mother. A gift I had taken for granted for forty-nine Christmases past.

I came home and checked my email. There was an email from Mitch Albom. A couple of days earlier—when we had spoken—before I could even find a way to comfortably get my mom's request from my brain to my mouth, Mitch volunteered, "Maybe I could write a little something for your mom. Would she like that?"

Would she like that? How did he know? I didn't even have to ask. "I mean, you don't have to do anything crazy. Nothing too long. Maybe just a paragraph or two saying that she was a nice lady and that she will be missed. I know you're so busy. Wow, yes, she would like that. She would really, really like that. But please don't go out of your way . . ."

"Lisa, I'd be happy to do it," he said.

And here, upon my arrival home, in my inbox, as requested by my mom, was the eulogy. As I read through it, tears washed over my cheeks. Millie Goich was loved. And I sure was blessed to have amazing friends like Mitch in my life.

Carla, the hospice aide, was finishing up her evening duties. My mom was clean, the TV was on, it was almost time for bed. After walking Carla to the front door and thanking her for being so kind to my mom, I went back into the family room and sat by my mom's bedside. She looked so pretty. Her hair had been washed, her face cleaned. Her curls framed her face and we smiled at one another.

"I'm glad you got out of your pajamas," she said.

"Well, these are technically pajamas," I said, referring to the outfit I bought at Target that afternoon.

"But you could wear those outside. And they're cute." She said, as if it was just any other day that I had brought clothes home for her to see.

"Do you like these slippers?" I asked, pointing at my high-top red knit slippers lined in faux lamb's wool.

"Those look very warm," she said.

"They are! Want to wear them?"

"No. My feet are under so many blankets, I don't need slippers. My socks are fine. You're so pretty," she added.

"I look just like you, Mother," I said. She touched my face and I closed my eyes feeling the warmth of her hand on my cheek. A comforting gesture I never wanted to end. I wanted to keep her hand there forever. To feel that touch every day.

"Mother, guess what? Mitch emailed your eulogy to me."

She perked up, eyes widening, with an expression of, "Well, what did he say?" on her face.

"Want me to read it to you?"

"Read it! Read it!" she exclaimed, like she had just received a return letter from her teen idol.

I began, "Millie—Although these are difficult last days, I have no doubt where you are going next. You'll be in heaven with a first class ticket . . ."

My mom's eyes filled with tears. Mine followed.

"In case you are overwhelmed by the beauty when you arrive and you find yourself temporarily speechless, here is a piece of paper that you can present to whoever is manning the gates, OK?"

I couldn't finish. I had to stop. I couldn't choke the words out and didn't want her to see me falling apart. I'd read the rest to her in the morning. I folded the letter in half and placed it on the table in front of the window.

"We'll finish this tomorrow, Mother."

"That's a good idea, honey," she said, wiping a tear from my cheek with the sleeve of her nightgown.

And we sat for the remainder of the evening, holding hands and watching TV until my mom fell asleep.

Day 9

"Love and joy come to you . . ."

My parents had an alarm in their house for probably fifteen years. And for that fifteen years, my mom had very strict rules about the alarm. Specifically, she was the armer and disarmer. This was her job. I don't know if she distrusted the rest of us to carry out this high security task, or if she just liked to do it because she liked to do everything in the house. She wasn't a delegator. Like the last waitress to leave the restaurant each night, or the flight attendant doing the final crosscheck on the plane, my mom was in charge of closing up the house before bed. The alarm normally was turned on after whatever

Lifetime movie my parents just finished watching. Which was usually around 11 p.m. They always felt safer watching the evening news, and certainly the *Tonight Show*, knowing that no one could penetrate the barrier that was encircling their encampment. "Instant!" she'd yell from the alarm panel in her bedroom. This meant that the instant alarm was on and—under no circumstances—should anyone open the door. Or else. This system worked great as my mom was normally the first to wake in the morning, so—in reverse—she'd disarm the alarm, yell, "Off!" and we all knew we were free to come and go as we pleased.

But this morning, momentarily forgetting that the official disarmer was officially incapacitated, at 7:45 a.m., my dad opened the door to bring the garbage cans in. Monday was garbage day and as it was my dad's job to bring in the bins from the curb, it was normally my mom's job to instruct him to do so. With the days running into each other and the pain medications beginning to dirty up my mom's normally crystal clear mind, my dad just went for it. And the whole neighborhood knew we were up. Even Kitty Finazzo.

My heart raced as I jumped out of bed at the sound of the bullhorn screaming through the house. My sister and I nearly collided in the hallway while both running out of our rooms to see what was wrong. And my mom, from her throne in the family room, was coherent enough to get out some of her favorite words, "Jesus Christ, Nick! What the hell did you do? God damn it! Turn the goddamned alarm off!" As I scrambled to remember the code in this panicked state, the phone rang. I answered. It was the alarm company. I told them it was a false alarm and they asked me for the secret password, which would alert them to the fact that I wasn't an intruder.

"What's the secret word?!?" I yelled from the kitchen.

"Goddamn it!" yelled my mom from her bed.

"Goddamn it is the secret word?!?" I asked.

I heard the woman on the phone chuckle slightly at the Laurel & Hardy sketch unfolding before her ears.

"Buffy. The secret word is Buffy!" yelled my dad. An homage to our former and beloved Cocker Spaniel. Like I should know that. Obviously.

"Buffy," I told the woman from the alarm company, and we were off the hook and free from arrest.

I couldn't help but laugh at what had just happened. I know it pissed my mom off as much as someone hopped up on Vicodin could be. And it was just one more example of how we needed Millie Goich in our lives in order for our lives to run smoothly. At four-foot-whatever she was, she would always be our leader.

My mom was agitated today. Surely the alarm had something to do with it, but clearly the end stage of her disease was near. Again, textbook. Everything the hospice nurse predicted would happen was unfolding as the days turned into nights turned into days. Up until this point, my mom's pain was controlled with Vicodin. We would administer a tablet every four hours or so and she seemed to be comfortable. Every morning the question would be, "Is today the day we give her the morphine?"

"Mother, do you want to start the morphine today?" we'd ask.

"No! I don't want morphine. I don't need it!" she'd protest.

My niece Sara, the doctor, warned us that the moment the morphine started was the moment we'd lose her. She would still be with us physically, but the rest of her mind and body would slip into a gentle drug-induced fog. She would no longer be lucid, her speech patterns would slow and conversation, for the most part, would gradually cease. Was I ready for that? Was I ready to stop hearing my mom's voice? Was I prepared to never have a conversation with my mom again? No. I wasn't. And neither was my mom.

My sister and the hospice nurse had a different take on it. They felt morphine needed to be started today. I wasn't going to be the one to administer it, so my sister took on that responsibility. We fought. I accused her of being a little too eager to start a medication that would render our mother basically comatose. She saw it as a dose of mercy.

"You're killing her, Kristina, you know that, right?" I said, accusingly.

"I'm not killing her. I'm administering *comfort*. Comfort, Lisa. Now give me the box."

I tried not to have this argument within earshot of my mom, but I know she heard us. I'm sure she was scared, and us bickering over the administration of the drug wasn't helping matters any.

With the nurse overseeing, I got "The Box" out of the refrigerator. I flipped open the lid and looked for the small bottle that said Morphine. I handed the bottle to my sister who unscrewed the top, pulling the required amount of the narcotic into a syringe and placing it under my mom's tongue. When the first syringe-full was administered, we held our breaths. And we all stared at my mom watching to see what would happen when the liquid made its way into her bloodstream. The agitation stopped, she looked calm. Not drunk or out of it—simply calm. She could move her legs again, something she hadn't been able to do in days. And she looked at us and smiled. And we exhaled. And for the first time in days my mom seemed to be at peace. The hospice nurse was right. It was time. And bless my sister for being the one to take on this heroic task.

My dad sat on the couch just looking at my mom. As I sat across from him, watching him hold her hand, crying as he was speaking to her, I realized how important sticking it out is in life. He kept most of his thoughts to himself these two weeks. But I know they were in there popping up throughout the day, like the little rodents in the Whack-a-Mole game. Hammering each one over the head before they could make their way out of the hole. My dad mentally whacked and whacked all week. I didn't know how to raise conversations with him about what was happening. He had spoken to the social worker the hospice provided a couple of times and I think that helped him immensely. He spoke to the chaplain. So he wasn't without guidance those last few days or without an ear to hear his story and concerns. Losing your life partner of over half a century is like losing yourself. They were a single unit. Inseparable. But certainly not without cracks.

My parents never had an Ozzie and Harriet type of relationship. Their communication style leaned more in the direction of Rush Limbaugh confronting an angry caller than that of a TV mom and dad. There wasn't a whole lot of, "Oh Mike! Oh Carol!" *Brady Bunch* conversations going on in our house over the years. Even a month before my mom died, she stood in the kitchen shaking saying, "I can't take it anymore! I can't take it! He just never stops yelling at me!" Yet for all of the tumult, there was an incredible sixty-four-year love that bubbled underneath it all.

Nick Goich and Millie Birach met at a weenie roast in April of 1947. My mom reiterated the story in her final days, with a sparkle in her eye and my dad's hand on her lap. It was an event put on by the *Yugo Forward* club—a social organization for people of Yugoslavian heritage. My mom actually attended with another guy named Pete. When she arrived at the picnic, my dad saw her walk in and, according to him, "That was it." Love at first sight. Pete didn't stand a chance. Later that evening as they were sitting around the fire on blankets, my dad walked over to my mom and said hello. During the conversation he told her, "I think I'm gonna marry you." My mom left with him that night, in his beat-up 1935 Ford, blowing off poor Pete, and the two of them never turned back. They were married in November, nine months later. My brother was born the following September. No time was wasted.

So now, more than six decades later, with Pete nothing more than a distant memory, these two who fell in love over weenies were saying goodbye to each other. My whole life—the trip to Cancun aside—I don't think they spent more than one or two nights apart from one another. They were always together. My dad was a factory worker and never traveled for business. My mother, a stay-at-home mom, was always there with dinner on the table when he came home from work. They vacationed together, they went to events together. I think of how different my life with my husband is. A traveling musician, more than half of our relationship has been spent being apart. I've learned to embrace independence. Something my mom and dad experienced as one. They were independently together.

My mom fell asleep and my sister and I took this time to go to the market around the corner to get some food for our dinner guests that evening. Mitch Albom and his producer—and my friend—Marc Rosenthal (Rosey as everyone called him), were stopping by after the radio show to say their goodbyes to my mom. We bought pasta and deli trays, olives and dips, chips and breads—our hunger, or perhaps our need to be doing something that wasn't waiting for our mother to die—filled our basket with just about everything we laid our eyes on. We came home and spread the food out on the dining room table. It was a feast for kings. I wish my mom could have seen it. She would have been so proud. She would have loved all of the food, too.

Mitch and Rosey arrived around 8:15 p.m. They ate very little but talked a lot. It was clear their single purpose was to spend time with my mom. Perhaps they felt guilty eating, or perhaps they just weren't hungry. My mom told Mitch how much she loved him. He, in return, told my mom that she was loved. Rosey made her laugh. We took a final picture of the three of them and, after an hour of goodbyes, they left with a deli tray and a nut roll in hand. Strict instructions from my mom. You leave empty-handed, you're on The Shit List.

My sister administered a second dose of morphine to my mom before bed. As she dozed off to sleep, we cleaned up the food, got ourselves ready for bed and spent the rest of the night in a pow wow in my sister's room.

"When do you think Mother's going to die?" I asked.

"I think it's going to be soon," said my sister, solemnly.

"Do you think she's going to feel it? I mean, is it going to hurt? Or will she be sleeping like she is now?"

"She'll probably be sleeping. And relaxed. The medicine will take care of the pain."

I tucked this information away as an assurance that her last minutes would be full of peace. I couldn't imagine it any other way.

Day 10

"Angels and archangels may have gathered there,
cherubim and seraphim thronged the air;
but his mother only, in her maiden bliss,
worshiped the beloved with a kiss . . ."

I always loved blow-drying my mom's hair. She had the best hair. It would go *exactly* where it was supposed to go—never a flyaway, never a curl that didn't cooperate perfectly. Her hair was thick with just the right amount of wave. A round brush and a blow dryer would be like clay in the hands of a potter. A little heat and, voilà, the perfect curl. I could never figure out why she would get perms. I did everything in my power since blow dryers were invented to straighten every curl on my head. For her to actually initiate *more* curls was perplexing to me. Whenever my mom had somewhere fancy to go—a wedding, a party, a funeral—she'd ask me to dry her hair for her and help her with her makeup. I loved making my mom look pretty.

In a few days, she would be going to the biggest event of her life. So this morning, I told her I wanted to pamper her one last time. I lined my mom's bed with plastic, brought in the pink wash pan the aides had been using, got some shampoo and propped the bin under her head. I used a glass to pour the water over her hair.

"Ooooooh, that feels good!" cooed my mom.

"I know, doesn't it? The best part of the haircut is always the shampoo. I'll massage your head for you. Is that good?"

She nodded.

As I massaged the shampoo into her head, she closed her eyes, smiling and lifting her eyebrows with each stroke of my hand. When we were finished, I placed the bin on the table, wrapped a towel around her hair, walked across the room and plugged the blow dryer into the outlet near my dad's rocking chair. Lifting her head gently from the plastic, I took her hair-filled round brush that she probably had for twenty-five years and wound the curls around the stiff bristles, making small waves from front to back. Getting the back styled was a challenge, but with a slight turn to the right, then to the left, she looked like she had just stepped out of the Paul Mitchell Salon. Normally, I'd give her a hand mirror to glance at the back of her head to see what it looked like, but without a mirror in front of her, it was a moot point. Tonight, she just went with the flow. Enjoying the hot air blowing on her head and the tactile love she was receiving. Even in death we want to feel beautiful.

"Next we're going to do your nails, Mother."

"Go get my polish in my room."

"Nope. I got something better."

I went to the drugstore earlier in the afternoon and picked out some nail polish for this final makeover. Rather than use the frosty white nail polish my mom had worn day after day, year after year for her entire life, I picked something out that I thought reflected her personality and was completely different than anything she would pick for herself: *Hot Pants Pink*. It made me happy and it made her happy, too. Perhaps on a day when she wasn't under the influence of narcotics and toxins coursing through her body, she would have said, "Oh, that's too bright for me!" But today, she embraced it.

My mom always had beautiful fingers and beautiful nails. Really long nail beds that I envied, that were so unlike my stumpy nails I had bitten most of my life. I held each finger in my hand as I glided the brush over her cold and bluing fingertips. The pink covered the darkness that was starting to pool in the end of her fingers. I wonder if this is why funeral homes paint the nails of people after they've gone. After the final pinky finger received its second coat, she rested her hands on her belly, the fuchsia sparkling brightly even against the nightgown she was wearing that had seen better days.

While her nails were drying I asked her a question I had been thinking about for a few days. "Mother, can you think of something really meaningful to leave behind for me? A message for me to live by and remember you by? A piece of wisdom you never want me to forget? I want to get a tattoo of the message right here on my wrist. So it's with me forever. You know, something profound."

My mom scrunched her nose, looked straight at me and with a *Hot Pants Pink* finger pointed in my direction and not a second of hesitation, said, "Don't get a tattoo, you'll get hepatitis."

I couldn't help but laugh. I was waiting for this profound motto to come out. Sage wisdom. And in true Millie Goich Queen Of Hypochondria fashion, I was left with, "Don't get a tattoo, you'll get hepatitis."

Not daring to push the request any further, I picked up the makeup brush and swept a little "rouge," as she always called it, over her porous cheekbones. Then, pulling the edge of her wrinkled eyelid to the side, I added a line of black eyeliner to the lash end of the lid, then did the same on the other side. A touch of gloss on her parched lips, she smacked them together when I asked her to blend the color in for me. I handed her the mirror and, when she caught the reflection of herself, she smiled.

"I look pretty."

"Yes, Mother. Yes, you do."

A satisfied customer. She turned her head from side to side, inspecting her hair as she always did. "Spray a little more back there," she asked. "Now a little more on the sides." Always a fan of hairspray, even on this last day of beauty, she still instructed me to "spray some extra so my hair doesn't flatten out in the back." And I did.

When we were finished, I brought the wash pan into the bathroom and rinsed it out in the tub, turning it over to dry. By the time I came back into the family room, my mom had already fallen asleep. Her eyeshadow peeking out from the folds and creases on her eyelids, she looked like she was simply taking a nap before going to the ball. I sat down next to her, watching her breathe, and wrote out the card I purchased a couple of days earlier for her pouch.

"Dear Mother," I began.

Don't open this card until you get to heaven. I want you to have something to read when you get there. Please know that I miss you already.

And every day of my life that goes by without you in it will be a little less full than when you were here. Thank you for being the best mother anyone could ever ask for. Thanks to you, I was never without a birthday party or an Easter dress. Thank you for never discouraging me from imagining. I never needed anything in my life when you were in it. You were my provider, my rock, my sounding board, my friend. Maybe I never told you, and maybe I should have told you more, but you were so good at being a mom. You perfected the art and elevated the job to a level only few reach. I love you more than I could ever express. Please continue to watch over me and I'll continue to talk to you. Listen for my words. I love you, Mother. Sleep well.

Lisa

I read the card one final time, running my hands over the embossed flowers on the cover, placed it in the bright yellow envelope, wrote my mom's name on the front, licked the envelope and kissed the card before sliding it into the center pocket of the pouch.

My sister stayed behind to look after her while my dad and I went to *The Mitch Albom Show*. Mitch had invited us to the studio the evening before, and it would be a great way to get my dad out of the house and his mind off what was unfolding before him. My dad loved going to the radio station. He got dressed up in his tan corduroy pants, put on a pullover sweater and his church shoes. He combed his hair and splashed his face with a little Old Spice cologne. I loved the Old Spice. One sniff and I was immediately transported back to my childhood, Sunday mornings, pre-church, with the smell of Old Spice, French toast and bacon in the air.

"You ready to go, Father?" I asked.

"Let's get a move on."

"You look handsome! Mother, look at Father. Doesn't he look nice?"

My mom, half awake, glanced over to my dad who was standing by her bedside, "Ohhhhhh, my Nicky. You'll always be the most handsome man to me."

My dad leaned down and kissed my mom goodbye. I did the same. And as my dad got in the Jeep and headed toward downtown Detroit, I thought of church and my mom and tried to wrap my head around how I was going finish my life without her. Would my dad become my new mom, or would that space just be left as a void forever? Would my dad still put his Old Spice on after my mom was gone? Or did he go that extra step for her? Would he know which sweater to wear with which pair of pants? My mom always got his outfits together for him. I guess we'd all figure it out at some point. But for now, she was alive, and we'd honor her by not changing a thing.

When we pulled onto West Grand Boulevard, the golden tower of the Fisher Building sparkled in the distance against the grey Michigan sky. A Detroit treasure since 1928, the Fisher Building housed WJR Radio, the station Mitch Albom broadcast his show from. WJR is known as the "The Great Voice Of The Great Lakes." A 50,000 watt class A clear channel station, it's one of the most powerful radio stations in the United States. While working with Mitch over the years, I never took for granted these two iconic structures that I was so blessed to be housed in daily.

I joined Mitch on air while my dad sat in the engineer's booth behind the glass. We didn't talk of life or death, but of topical news stories that were a refreshing diversion for both my dad and me. Meanwhile, at home, my sister had turned the radio on for my mom so she could hear me through the radio, on air, one last time.

"We're coming home soon, Mother!" I said over those 50,000 watts as we wrapped up that evening's show. She heard me, and beamed. I could feel it coming back through my microphone from across the city. I was content knowing that, in my life, I had made my mom proud.

Day 11

"Guardian Angels God will send thee, all through the night . . ."

MY MOM: Did someone just come in?

MY SISTER & ME: Why, what do you see?

MOM: The same man who was here earlier. In the suit coat. He looks like a doctor. He's holding a piece of paper.

US: Is he talking to you?

MOM: No. He's looking around, just looking around.

On Day 11 of my mom's fourteen-day journey, she saw two men standing at the foot of her bed. They were standing together, not saying anything to her. They just stood there "inspecting" the situation.

I don't know what I believe about the afterlife or heaven. Prior to this I had a single experience in college with a spirit that spooked me for many years to follow. But as I grew older, I became more skeptical. So did my mom. She wasn't necessarily a religious person, or a believer in ghosts or spirits. So when she started having conversations with "people," I listened. And listened carefully. I believe that what she saw was real. And I believe that someone came down to escort her to her new world, with her official passport to heaven in hand.

I had read that it wasn't unusual for dying people to interact with others who had passed in their final days. Most often it's someone they know; sometimes—as was the case with my mom—it was a stranger. Sometimes the interaction is joyful, sometimes quizzical. But to the person dying, who and what they're seeing is very real.

My mom saw the same man twice that day. At one point he was there with someone else; the next time he was alone. But it was the same person. Same description. She didn't seem to be hallucinating. She truly believed she was seeing someone. Maybe it's not until our bodies start failing that we can truly see the other side. Maybe once our body is half in this world and half in another—and we're weakened from illness— we allow the spirits in. Perhaps we're too firmly planted on this plane in our current life to interact with anyone else. Like a video game, we're not able to advance to the next level until we've performed a certain amount of tasks on this Earth.

I tried to get my mom on camera talking about these people. But every time I'd start the video, she would stop talking. Maybe this information isn't intended to be documented. Maybe the dying aren't supposed to tell us or we're not supposed to know. In which case, I probably heard enough. The man. The clipboard. His buddy. The foot of the bed. What more was there for me to be privy to? The part that was intriguing was that my mom said, "He's just looking around." Did he see me sitting there? Or did he only see my mom? Maybe the spirits could only see the dying. The clipboard probably contained my mom's information. Maybe height, weight, a photo of some sort. Stats and accomplishments on Earth. Maybe this gentleman was there to gather this information, a greeter sent down to assess the situation. Perhaps he, like an insurance adjustor, just came down to check out the scene. The business at hand.

He came down to see if she was truly ready to go. Then he went back "up there"—or wherever he was from—to meet with the angel bosses who would then send her official escort down a couple of days later.

I wondered who my mom's escort would be. Would it be my grandmother? Would it be a stranger? Maybe they would send my mom's sibling who died shortly after birth. Maybe it would be the "handsome gentleman" my mom had been talking about, the short one who made her smile.

One thing I knew for sure, someone was in the room with us. This wasn't a hallucination. She saw these gentlemen with her heart. That was enough to convince me that, indeed, they were present. My mom traveled in and out of consciousness the rest of the afternoon. I watched her sleeping and wondered what dreams were going on behind those closed eyes.

❄

My sister went to Cecilia's for a massage. While there, Cecilia told my sister she and her husband, Michael, wanted to do something special for my mom. They wanted to present her with a Native American name before her death. They would come over before the final hospice aide came for the night and asked my sister if it would be okay. Of course, my sister wholeheartedly accepted the visit.

That afternoon, my mom had been experiencing a lot of stomach pain. The morphine didn't seem to be helping—and we weren't quite sure it wasn't the cause. So we phoned hospice to have them send over a nurse. Tracey, the hospice nurse, arrived within the hour and determined that my mom's bladder was full and her stomach was bloating—a result of her kidneys not functioning—and put a catheter into my mom's bladder to relieve the pain.

"Millie, we're going to put a catheter in you," said Tracey, loud enough for my mom to hear. "It's going to be a little uncomfortable, but you're going to feel a whole lot better once we get some of this bad stuff out of your belly."

My mom's words were few at this point. "Okay," she weakly agreed.

And as Tracey cleaned the area, then slid the catheter into my mom's urethra, an enormous amount of urine began traveling through the clear plastic tube, pouring into the bag that hung from the rail of my mom's bed. It filled almost an entire bag within minutes, which had to be immediately changed and replaced with a new bag that would remain for the next couple of days. The relief my mom felt was immediate. The peace of mind we felt knowing she was being taken care of was priceless.

One step closer. One more symptom to check off the list.

Cecilia and Michael arrived around 7:30 p.m. Both came dressed in their ceremonial Native American clothing. Michael—Chief Medicinehawk—brought with him a beautiful handmade bracelet he crafted himself and an eagle feather. Cecilia gave my mom strings of beads. The feather was given to assist in her flight to the heavens. The bracelet would remain on her wrist from that night forward, traveling with her to the next life. The feather would go in her pouch along with the beaded necklaces. They gave her a full blessing ceremony, complete with chants and prayers, and bestowed upon her the name, *Princess Harvest Moon*. The name would signify her light and bountiful giving nature and would never be given to anyone else. They presented her with a framed certificate bearing her new name. My mom was touched beyond belief that someone would be doing this for her. Strangers, really. People who just did this out of the goodness of their souls. And she was elated with her new name.

"I'm a princess now?" she asked.

"Yes you are," said Cecilia. "It's official!"

"Wowwwwww. Who would have ever thought? Little old me. A *princess*! Isn't that something."

Tears flowed down all of our faces. Cecilia and Michael stayed for a bit, talked to my mom, then left, with my mom's heart overflowing.

The hospice worker arrived about a half hour later to clean my mom up for bed. Carla, the aide, took out my mom's dentures and soaked them in a cup full of blue mouthwash that was sitting on the coffee table. She changed my mom's diaper, slipped a clean pad underneath her hips, placed the oxygen hose back into my mom's nostrils and kissed my mom on the forehead telling her she'd see her the following night. My mom asked Carla if she could give her the feather to hold. Carla obliged, placing the feather in my mom's hand, closing her fingers around its stem. My mom told Carla to take some cookies home for her daughter.

Carla packed a Christmas-themed tin full of nut rolls and peanut butter balls and as she was on her way out the door, said, "Thank you, Princess Harvest Moon. I'll be looking for you in the sky." Carla knew that night, without letting on to my mom, that this would be the last time they'd see one another.

Mentally, my mom was still present, but I could see that things were starting to shift. She was sleeping more, communicating less and starting to wander off in her thoughts. She'd rally for a while but then her mind was transported to another place in time. It was as if she had one foot in the present, in her family room, and the other in the future, running through a green meadow, with our former family dog, Buffy, by her side. Yes, that Buffy. The cherished companion my parents' alarm system secret word was named after.

My mom's exit had been textbook. I knew that most likely within a day, our communication would cease. It's a very strange concept to know that within twenty-four hours you'll never hear this person speak again. While I still had her there, and she was still somewhat able to comprehend, I flipped through my mental Rolodex to think if there were any last-minute outstanding issues that needed to be discussed, words left unsaid, apologies that needed to be made. Yes. There was one. The Skyhawk Incident.

Whether or not I should to go there was the dilemma I faced that evening. For thirty-two years, my mom believed that "a goddamned woman at the golf course" had hit her beloved Buick Skyhawk. I never had the heart to tell her that I was the one who put the three-panel gouge in the passenger side of the car during an afternoon of fun, sun and boys with my girlfriends.

When I was in high school, my mom had a mid-life regeneration. As a stay-at-home mom since my brother was born thirty-one years prior, she hadn't held a job outside the home since she worked for the Yugoslav Embassy in her early twenties. At fifty-three, she decided she wanted to take a part time job to make a little money and see the outside world. She applied for a job at Dan's Donut Castle—my place of employment—and was hired. She was thrilled. This meant that she would need transportation to get to and from work, since my dad and I might not always be around to drive her. She hadn't driven a car since the death-defying incident back in 1962 with my Kuma Dorothy. But the fear had dissipated and she was ready to take her place behind the wheel. She brushed up on her driving with my dad, went to the Secretary of State, took her driving test, passed with flying colors and was now a working, driving, middle-aged woman on the go! She even began golfing. Which was also a post-menopausal surprise. I never knew my mom to be sporty at all. Unlike my Aunt Dolores who did everything from skiing to whitewater rafting, my mom was normally content with hobbies like crocheting and playing with her handheld slot machine. The thought of my mom whitewater rafting? Never. I never saw her step foot in a swimming pool or a lake the entire forty-nine years she was in my life. Perhaps it was the time as a teenager that her canoe tipped over in the middle of the Detroit River and she nearly drowned that did it. We'll never know. But this new golf epiphany was a curveball to all of us.

One day, my parents were out for the day and my girlfriends called to ask if I wanted to go to the Cider Mill. Yates Cider Mill was a place we all went to hang out while we were in high school. It was a place to meet boys from other schools, drink cider (occasionally laced with alcohol), hang out and have a good time. My mom's car was the only one available that day. I was never supposed to take it without permission, but in this case I figured I'd go for an hour or two, have the Skyhawk back before they arrived home and they'd never know I had taken it. Teenage mistake number one: Never test the lying-to-your-parents gods. The gods always win.

As we were exiting to leave the Cider Mill, our car had been blocked in on all sides by the cars of other partying teens. We couldn't locate the people whose cars were haphazardly parked around ours, so my friends had a genius idea to "guide me" out of my spot. I hadn't even had my driver's license a full year at this point. So a skilled driver, I was not. With my friends' instructions to "pull forward, now go backward, stop, turn to the left, no stop, turn to the right, now go straight back . . . NO! Straight back!"

KRRRRRRRRRRRRRRRRRRRRRSSSSSSSSSCCHHHHHHHHH.

The passenger side of the Skyhawk scraped against the side of a pickup truck. It sounded like someone had taken a knife to the side of the car. Since I had never been in an accident before, I wasn't quite sure what the noise meant, but I knew that whatever was happening couldn't have been good. And from the looks on my girlfriends' faces who were now silent on the other side of the glass, I knew my assumptions were probably correct.

"Is everything okay out there?" I asked hesitantly, knowing what the answer was.

"Ummmm, well . . ." responded my friend Vicki, with a look on her face that said, "Not okay. Not okay at all."

I stepped out of the car, walked around to the passenger side and felt my heart splash into my stomach. Poor Skyhawk. Poor me. The passenger side was gouged across all three panels. The truck didn't seem to sustain any damage at all, but my little yellow banana was screwed. And so was I. How would I tell my mom and dad? I wasn't even supposed to have the car! Oh, boy. I was in trouble.

We sped home (probably not a good idea, considering), and opened the automatic garage door to reveal *no car inside.* My parents weren't home yet. Brilliant. This would buy me more time to make up a story. Orrrrrrr . . . was a story even necessary at this point? With the car safely back in the garage and no knowledge of me even taking it out that afternoon, my genius seventeen-year-old brain said to itself, "Don't say anything! Just leave it there! Silence now. Think later." And that's what I did. I left the car in the garage, went into the house, and never said a word.

For three excruciatingly stressful weeks I waited for my mom or dad to say something. Nothing. Until that sunny afternoon when my mom stopped off at the Donut Castle after a round of golf earlier that morning with her women's league. I was working behind the counter when I saw the Skyhawk pull up in front of the building. With the passenger side facing the store window, I could see the sun bouncing off of the scratch that looked worse to me now than it had the day it happened. Guilt seemed to make it ten inches deeper than it was. My mom sat down for awhile, chatted a bit with the regulars over a cup of coffee, then turned to leave. As she walked out into the parking lot, I saw her stop next to the car. Staring. In silence. Then I saw her arms flying up in the air. I saw her mouthing something. I saw the S-word. I saw the F-word. I saw another S-word. She grabbed her head, turned on her heel, and stomped into the donut shop. Oh, F-word. The jig is up.

"I can't believe that one of those goddamned ladies at the golf course hit my car today and just left without saying anything! Look at it! The whole side is smashed. Goddamned women! Who hits someone's car and doesn't leave a note?! Oh, your father is not going to be happy about this. I'm calling the golf course when I get home."

And for the next thirty-two years, that was the story. A "goddamned lady at the golf course" hit her car. And on this, the eleventh day of her fourteen-day journey, I readied myself to tell her the truth.

As I held her hand, I prefaced the admission by telling her how much I loved her. I'm sure she could feel my pounding heart through my fingertips. What seemed like an hour of silence passed before I finally got up the nerve to say, "Remember that time the Skyhawk got smashed?"

She interrupted my confession by looking lovingly into my eyes. She brushed my bangs off my forehead and let her hand linger on my cheek. "You're such a good girl. You've always been such a good girl," she said, as a tear made its way down my face, settling in the corner of my mouth.

I took a deep breath and said, "That goddamned woman at the golf course."

She nodded her head and we left it at that.

Day 12

"Christmas Eve is coming soon, now, you dear old man,
Whisper what you'll bring to me: Tell me if you can . . ."

The nurse taking my mom's vitals this morning said, based on the numbers, my mom had about twenty-four to forty-eight hours left to go. Twenty-four. Forty-eight. Of all the hours in all the days I've spent with my mom, I was down to the last handful. How do you maximize time when these numbers are put on paper? You feel the need to fill each sixty seconds of each sixty minutes of each one of those twenty-four to forty-eight hours with something meaningful. What ultimately happens is, you realize that meaningful is simply sitting still with that person and surrounding yourself with their existing life force.

The nurse gave my dad a pamphlet to read on the signs of death:

1. Loss of appetite. *Check.*

2. Excessive fatigue and sleep. *Check.*

3. Increased physical weakness. *Check.*

4. Mental confusion or disorientation. *Check. Check.*

5. Labored breathing. *Check.*

6. Social Withdrawal. *Check.*

7. Changes in urination. *For days now.*

8. Swelling in the feet and ankles. *Check.*

9. Coolness in the tips of fingers and toes. *Freezing.*

10. Mottled veins and splotchy skin. *Checkmate.*

They also mentioned the "death rattle." It sounds just like it sounds. A rattling from the back of the throat caused by an excess accumulation of saliva in the throat and lungs. Unable to clear it themselves, it pools in the throats of the dying, filling the room with the ancient sounds of impending death.

Then there was the surge of energy as death gets nearer. The dying may want to get out of bed if they are mobile, talk more than usual or ask for food, days after having no appetite. I've seen it in my animals who have passed, and it was happening with my mom. She requested breakfast this morning, for the first time since she had been home. We gave her some eggs, a half a piece of toast and some juice. She ate it as if it was just a normal day. For a few minutes we were all hopeful that perhaps the tides were turning. Could it be possible that she was getting *better*? That she wouldn't die? That she would live now, after all? As quickly as the surge began, however, it crashed. Like a hurricane had just blown through my mom, leaving the eye behind—the calm before the storm.

From my dad's journal entry that day:

My weight (160) BP (105-85-63) Sugar (126). I read the hospice pamphlet on the signs of death. I have oatmeal.

Completely nonchalant. Squeezing signs of death in between his blood sugar reading and his oatmeal. Like it's all in a day's work.

As I was washing the breakfast dishes, I heard the clattering of the mailbox opening on the porch. John The Mailman had arrived with the day's goods in his bag. We always referred to him by his name and title. Never just simply, John. When I heard the familiar drop, I stepped outside to tell him about my mom's situation. John The Mailman has been my parents' mail carrier for twenty-five years. When you're in your eighties, the mailman is more than just a guy who puts junk mail in your box. He's an event. A daily ritual that signals a specific time of day. With him comes things to do: Bills to pay. Cards to read. Business to tend to. My parents saw their mailman differently than I see mine. To them, John The Mailman was family. And I couldn't let a family member not participate in my mom's farewell celebration.

I asked John The Mailman if he'd come in for a minute to say goodbye to my mom. He said he'd be honored, and leaving his big bag of mail by the front door, I felt the cold bounce off of his blue United States Postal Service coat as he stamped his snow-filled shoes on the front rug and walked through the kitchen. He stopped at the top of the single stair as he caught first sight of my mom. My dad motioned John The Mailman to come to the bed. My mom looked up, smiled for the first time that morning, and grabbed John The Mailman's hand. They talked for awhile about Christmas and family and holiday plans and vacations.

My mom motioned my dad toward the kitchen, instructing him to "Give John his Christmas money."

John The Mailman let out a nervous giggle at the suggestion, and shrugged off the envelope when my dad handed it to him. "No, no, no . . . that's okay," insisted John The Mailman.

My mom would have nothing of the rebuff, "You better take it, or I'll haunt you from the other side!"

John The Mailman laughed, tapped my mom's forehead lovingly with the envelope, then placed it in the top pocket of his sweater.

My mom probably filled this card out in October. She was organized like that. The calendar on the kitchen counter was marked with birthdays and stars, with cards purchased a year ahead of time, filled out in advance, hidden between the calendar's pages. John The Mailman was family, after all, and held a special place in between these sacred pages, too.

John The Mailman said he had to be on his way. With Christmas three days away, his mailbag runneth over.

"Bundle up," my mom added as she grabbed his hand for the final time. Through tears, John The Mailman said he would, and left with a pile of Christmas cards in hand to deliver to others having a much different holiday than this little house on the corner would be having this year.

❄

The afternoon was still. There were a couple of hours where no guests arrived; only my mom, dad, sister and I were at home. So I sat in the family room with my mom, basking in her final minutes of life. At this point, there weren't a lot of words being exchanged between the two of us. At least not verbally. The words between us were now communicated through our eyes. The surge had subsided and my mom was back to a restful state. Suddenly, this snapshot hit me as a stark reminder that I would never have this moment to share with a daughter of my own. I'd never be able to use the name "Ruby" that I have been coveting for so many years. Who would hold *my* hand when I was dying? Panic set in.

Not having children is my biggest regret in this lifetime. I married late in life (at thirty-eight, which is late for a girl, I suppose). My husband said from the beginning that he didn't want children, but I always thought I could change his mind. My mom always told me you could never change a man's mind and never change a man. "No matter how strong your love is, or how persuasive you are—listen to the words your man tells you and *believe* them. They speak the truth. You. Will. Not. Change. Him." And, as usual, she was right.

The no kids thing didn't bother me at the beginning. The freedom I had—that my girlfriends didn't—convinced me that perhaps I had made the right decision. But as menopause peeked at me from around the corner, my regret became deeper. I saw friends of mine sending their children off to college, walking them down the aisle and their children having children of their own. The pain was sometimes so immensely unbearable I had to force it out of my head.

I was pregnant once. A one-night stand with an ex-boyfriend. We were both new to Los Angeles, just starting to pursue our comedy careers on the West Coast and we hooked up for old-time's sake. I knew from the moment of impact that I was with child. I can't explain it. I don't know how I knew. I just knew. At the time I still carried a torch for my ex. So for me the choice was clear: we get back together, have this baby and see where the road takes us.

His choice was quite different. He insisted I not keep the baby. Fortunately, I never had to make that decision, the decision was made for me. Three months after I found out I was pregnant, I had a miscarriage. An awful, painful, near-nervous-breakdown-inducing miscarriage. When it happened, the one thing that kept me sane was the thought that perhaps one day I'd have a second chance at the baby thing. Or a third chance. But, as life rolled on, it never happened.

Many years later I ran into my ex at the mall. We hadn't seen each other in over ten years. He took out his iPhone and showed me pictures of his children. Two perfect little boys. That hurt. I could feel my uterus weeping for the loss of these boys' half-sibling. And it all came crashing down on me as I sat with my mom, in silent reverie.

It's because I had such a great role model in my own mother, that I wanted to be a mother myself one day. She made mothering look easy. She made being a child fun. My mom was the Steve Jobs of mothers. I wish I had the chance to follow in her footsteps.

My mom settled down for a nap, and so did I. While sleeping, my brother and his family had arrived for the day. The noise of their arrival woke me. Lying in bed, watching the cat mobile on the ceiling dancing as the air from the furnace spun their balls of yarn around in circles, I listened to my family gathered around the dining room table talking and eating down the hall. I could hear forks on plates. Porcelain against table. Cupboards opening and closing. Aluminum foil being removed from the tops of casserole dishes. Footsteps against the linoleum floor. But what I didn't hear was my mom's voice. Her unique footsteps. Scurrying around the kitchen, making sure everyone was being taken care of. The absence of my mom's sounds was deafening to me. It sucked the din of the rest of the family right out of the air and left the room mute. But I knew that to my mom's ears, hearing her family together was pure joy. And for the first time in two weeks, I had a complete meltdown. Big. Long. Hard. Heaving. Punching my pillow, cursing life. Cursing death. I cried in my bed like I had so many times over the years. But this time it wasn't a boy, or a fight with a girlfriend who opened the floodgates. It was my heart that finally got the message from my brain that my mom would no longer be with us.

The thought of this immediately propelled me out of bed. Barely acknowledging my family, I stepped down into the family room and sat at my mom's side. I continued weeping without words. Just wept. As I did, I saw a tear roll down the side of her face and into the maze of her right ear.

I hated crying in front of her. I tried to remain strong throughout these two weeks. In fact, I'd even go so far as to say there was a nonchalance about the whole situation. A sort of, "Well, it is what it is and we just have to deal with it, right?" Though I thought all along this was for her protection, perhaps it was really for my own.

The doorbell rang. Cecilia, who, a day earlier, had blessed my mom with her princess name, came back to give my mom a massage. My mom had never had a professional massage in her life. "I don't want anyone touching me!" she'd say. But tonight, perhaps it was the morphine or the fact that she simply couldn't fight it any longer, she acquiesced. For ninety minutes, Cecilia oiled and kneaded my mom's tiny arms, legs, twisted spine and head. The contentment that was on my mom's face when the massage was over was something I had never seen before.

Cecilia leaned over to my mom and said, "Millie, we're all done." And my mom smiled like she was drunk and said, "Why did I wait eighty-five years to get a massage?"

"I've been saying that to you forever, Mother! Now you know why I enjoy them so much."

"What that could have done for my back all these years. I never knew."

Then she added the kicker that went straight for my stomach, "Lisa, make sure you get Cecilia's card so I can have her come back after you leave."

Tears.

I wanted to say, "Mother, you realize you're going to die in a couple of days, right? There will be no 'after I leave.'" But instead I said, "Yes, Mother, I'll get her card and put it on the buffet in the kitchen.

Her first and last massage complete, she fell asleep with a smile on her face.

Day 13

"Above thy deep and dreamless sleep,
the silent stars go by . . ."

Mika is restless—doesn't want to be bothered. We go to Kaul's Funeral Home to make all final arrangements for Mika's burial. Then we have snacks/ribs/cheese/pop.

My dad's journal entry for the day, once again, was filled with juxtaposition. Going from planning a funeral to having snacks. Perhaps it was his way of avoiding what was just around the corner.

This was a challenging morning. My mom was extremely uncomfortable and none of us knew what to do to make her better. It was difficult to reason with her because her mind was elsewhere at this point.

One of the stages of dying involved "picking." The hospice nurses told us to expect this. They said it could be a sign of less oxygen available to the brain or distress due to pain, nausea, constipation or a full bladder. It could also be due to being confused or anxious about something. My mom experienced this stage today. She picked at her nightgown all morning, nearly tearing it off herself. We calmly tried to hold her arms down, telling her that she was in a safe place and that everything would be okay. But the agitation continued. It wasn't until we administered another dose of morphine that her hands unclenched and her arms fell into a resting position. It was so hard watching her go through this pain. It was the worst she had been throughout this almost two-week period.

After the narcotic had settled into my mom's bloodstream and she had finally fallen asleep, my dad, brother, sister and I left for the funeral home to begin planning for my mom's burial. What a family outing this was. She was still alive, after all, and here we all were, wearing our fancy clothes and piling into a car to plan the rest of her week that would be happening in one, two, maybe three days from now.

Pulling into the back of the funeral home, we parked behind a hearse. This brought it all home. My mom would be in the back of this hearse—or perhaps another one just like it—in a matter of days. Right now she was at home, though. Living. Breathing. Picking. But soon we'd all be following behind this car, flags waving in the wind, tissue wadded up in our hands, wearing our black dresses, while friends and family members trailed behind us, their tears mixing with ours.

As we stepped out of the car we were greeted by Jack, the funeral director. He shook my dad's hand, then my brother's, then reached in to give my sister and me a hug. Jack is an old family friend. I had once dated his son, Stephen. Stephen and I spent a week together in the Cayman Islands. My mind started wandering back to that vacation—and the diving and dining and beach walking under the Caribbean sun—but I immediately pulled my focus back to the moment, tucking away memories of an old love for another day. A more appropriate time. Only interacting with Jack in social situations over the years, it was strange seeing him here, in this surrounding, actually doing his job. It's sort of like your friends who are your friends in the real world, then going to work with them and seeing how they spend the rest of their days. Two different people. Two different lives.

As Jack walked us through the funeral home—a pretty place done in dark greens and floral prints—the smell of flowers, both fresh and rotting, brought back memories of previous goodbyes.

"This is the room Millie will be in," he said, pointing through two double doors to the right. The room was large and long. In the front of the room sat a brass stand. Now empty, soon to be topped with my mom's casket. Flanking the stand were pillars of various heights that would be draped with floral arrangements in the coming days with ribboned banners saying things like, "Beloved Mother," "Dear Grandmother," "Cherished Friend."

Rows and rows of upholstered chairs filled the room. Off to the sides were separate, smaller seating areas where people would gather, sharing their stories of my mom and her life and everything she meant to them.

"How many people does this room hold?" asked my brother.

"About three hundred," replied Jack. "Although, we can accommodate spillover into the room next door or the smaller rooms across the hall.

My sister and I remained silent, taking it all in, occasionally glancing at one another with an "I don't like any of this" look on our faces.

My brother assessed the situation. He was the ringleader for the funeral portion of this death extravaganza. Richard walked through the room, planning where the church choir would sing during the memorial service, where the podium would be positioned for the eulogy, where the family would gather to receive guests. I was grateful he was taking the reins—this area certainly wasn't my strong suit. I was much more comfortable diapering my mother than I was planning logistics for a funeral.

Jack guided the four of us to a room down the hall, in what looked to be the lunch room. We all sat around a small wooden table. There were sinks, a refrigerator and vending machines, along with several other tables and chairs. The decor was country, more dark green carpeting and antique, flowered wallpapered walls. Little knick-knacks were placed around the room, giving the feeling that you were in someone's home. It did serve the purpose of making it familiar and comforting. But in the end, it was still a funeral home.

Angie came with us, sitting quietly in her carry bag at my side, oblivious to the pomp and circumstance unfolding around her. My sister and I sat near each other, with the three men sitting across from us at the table.

"The first thing we need to do is pick out a casket," Jack said.

He respectfully placed the casket catalog in front of us and opened it to a page. As a lifelong catalog shopper, this was a new one for me. When someone is still alive, it doesn't seem quite right to be looking through a casket catalog. But it's what you do as the end draws near so that it doesn't have to be done when you're in that deep state of mourning. It's easier this way, they say.

"Here, these are lovely," he said, pointing to metallic monstrosities that looked as though they would swallow my now sixty pound mother whole.

"How much is that casket?" I asked.

"That casket is $8,000. But it's superior quality and will last for all of eternity."

"In the ground," I added dryly. "Where no one will ever see it."

"Well, you're putting your mother in her final home. Her final resting place. I think you'd want it to be nice." I wasn't sure if the slight twinge of guilt I was feeling was laced in his statement, or was coming from my own self-infliction.

My sister and I flipped through the pages and both—at once— pointed to the same, simple, wooden casket. Both of us being creative types, I think we admired the simple straight lines of the casket, which starkly contrasted the palatial gold-encrusted examples on the pages prior. It was mid-century modern versus Palace of Versailles.

"I like this one!" I said, enthusiastically.

"Me, too," added my sister.

My dad and brother just sat, probably overwhelmed by the process, letting the girls do their shopping.

Jack immediately interjected, "Oh, you don't want that casket. It's made of fiberboard. It's a (whispering) welfare casket. It's for people who don't have a lot of money."

A welfare casket? That was a thing? I wasn't sure exactly what that meant, but we didn't have a lot of money, either. And I was sure my mom would prefer spending $1,000 instead of $8,000 for a box that would house her bones that no one would ever see. With some flowers on top of the box, and a nice silk lining and pillow inside, I thought it would make a lovely resting place. Simple. Clean. Unassuming. Just like my mother.

But the "welfare casket" line stuck in our heads and we ended up going with a powder blue model with brushed stainless steel handles. It was $4,250. My sister and I didn't like it very much, but my brother and dad did. In the end, we figured it would match the dress we picked out for my mom. The handles would match her shoes. That alone would make my mom happy.

We tied up the rest of the logistics and loose ends, from details on the funeral procession to final costs for renting out the viewing room. Jack presented my father with an itemized invoice, which my dad signed and handed back to Jack. Part one of funeral planning day was now behind us.

From the funeral home, we drove to the cemetery to alert them that my parents' plots would finally be put to use. My parents had purchased a four-for-two deal on these plots over a decade earlier. Because my family tends to embrace morbidity, we would often take Sunday drives to look at the grass where they would one day reside. My dad would say, "There's our future home, Mika!" Almost excited. Like it was a beach house in the Florida Keys. Sometimes we'd get out of the car and stand on the grass and look around, pointing out the panoramic view from the property. The plots were located in a beautiful part of the Eastern Orthodox section of the cemetery, amongst other Serbians, Greeks and Russians. A curve in the road led to their spot, just off the path, and was easily accessible from the road. It was really tranquil here. A piece of real estate we could all hope to retire to one day.

Though we drove by the plots that afternoon, we didn't get out of the car because it had been sleeting and wet. So we went into the office, met with the caretaker and discussed the approximate day of burial and funeral plans. Once these were in place, we headed back home to tell my mom that everything was settled.

We told her about the blue casket and the silver handles. We told her about the headstone we would order with the slot machine emblem embossed under her name, to mark for all eternity her favorite pastime. We told her that she was going to be well cared for and we would make sure that her final party was a good one.

❄

We're waiting for Mika to fall asleep, my dad continued in his journal.

Of course, "fall asleep" didn't mean doze off. He was referring to the big sleep. The final sleep. The sleep where his Mika would be lying next to him no more. I wondered at this moment if this scared my dad.

I'm not afraid of dying. I've often said, I'm more afraid of living than of dying. The thought of living forty years beyond retirement frightens me to the core. I've never been a good saver. Conversely, I've been an *excellent* spender. As my mom would say often after I moved to Los Angeles, "If you spent as much time looking for a job as you did roller-blading, you'd be a millionaire." And she was right. The nine months of rollerblading I enjoyed after first moving to Venice Beach in 1996 broke me. But my legs looked *great*!

If my mom feared death in those final days, she didn't really show it. She would often say, "I'm gonna miss you when I go up there."

Which always melted my heart, because she seemed sure that there really was an "up there" to go to. That was encouraging. As a woman who wasn't particularly religious in her life, this gave me some sort of solace that she had faith there was something else after she left this place. And it helped to give me a little faith, too. There was no question she was going to a really nice somewhere. A place where we'd all meet again one day for a picnic. Everyone who stopped by in those last days was invited to my mom's "picnic." Oh, how I hope there's a picnic to go to. I'm about as good of a believer as I am a saver. I want so much to believe. Maybe when it's my time to die, I'll be planning my own picnic, too.

In the booklet *A Time To Live*, Hospice Nurse Barbara Karnes writes, "When it comes time to die, we are all going to be afraid to some degree. Because few people talk about dying or tell us what it's like to die, we don't know what to expect. There comes a time when you'll wonder, 'Am I going to die today? Is today the day?' If you can ask that question, then you are probably not going to die that day. The day you die, you won't ask and you won't care."

My mom didn't seem to care. In fact, she was getting antsy toward the end when she *wasn't* dying. When the hospice nurse arrived on her last morning she took my mom's blood pressure.

MY MOM TO HOSPICE NURSE: How was my blood pressure this morning?

NURSE: It was perfect!

MY MOM: Shit.

She was ready to go. And she didn't know why the man at the end of her bed wasn't taking her.

❋

As the day progressed and the moon pushed the sun from the sky, my mom simply stopped talking. She had a last-minute rally in the morning, then just crashed. I don't remember her last words to me and that makes me sad. I guess I just thought she was falling asleep and we'd continue our conversation when she woke up. So I never made a point to remember what we last talked about. She never made it back to this world. Though she was conscious, she was just staring at the ceiling for the next several hours. She was shutting down. Her eyes were wide open and her mouth hung slack-jawed. I would try to close her eyes, but they'd pop back open, black and empty. I tried putting droplets of water into her mouth—hoping not to choke or drown her—so she could get some hydration. Did hydration even matter at this point? Probably not. But it made me feel better to be taking care of her, rather than know I was just watching her slip away.

Even though she was unresponsive, we all continued to talk to her throughout the day. We told her we loved her a thousand and one times. And we never let go of her hand. My Aunt Dolores, said not to ask them questions, because answering the questions puts too much stress on the dying. Since hearing is the last of the senses to go, doctors believe that those near death can hear us, want to respond, but can't. I'm not sure how they know this if the patient can no longer communicate, but maybe it's the same research that tells scientists that flies can't focus or that dogs feel jealousy. It's fact that needs to be trusted. I needed to test this theory myself. Just looking at my mom, she looked like a shell. It looked as if there was no brain activity whatsoever, other than what was keeping her heart beating and her breaths flowing in and out. I leaned over to my mom's ear and whispered, "If you can hear me, don't worry about trying to talk, just squeeze my hand. Just squeeze my hand." I had seen that plenty of times in the movies and thought it might be worth a shot tonight. In less than a minute, she squeezed my hand. I squeezed hers back. Knowing she could indeed hear me, I never stopped talking to her until the minute she took her last breath.

As a family, we decided to cancel the social worker for the evening since my mom was unresponsive and we didn't want to cause any unnecessary stress to her body. "Just let her rest," we said. And she remained at rest, with the open eyes and the open mouth and the "Ker Phhhhhhh" of the air mattress keeping her blood circulating through her veins.

Day 14

"Sleep in heavenly peace. Sleep in heavenly peace."

We all sat vigil into the early morning hours of December 24th, keeping watch over my precious mother. My brother, my sister, my dad and me. We decided to take shifts so that my mom would not be alone. We knew that the moment was near, and we didn't want her making the transition without us. My dad had fallen asleep on the couch with Angie sleeping on his chest. The eye shades my sister bought my dad for Christmas shielded his vision from the sadness going on around him. He needed to sleep. We told him we'd wake him up if my mom's condition changed. Her breathing had slowed, as the hospice worker said it would. Her mouth had been open most of the night—along with her eyes—staring blankly at nothing, or perhaps something, we couldn't see. As the moment drew nearer, her mouth began to close, making it appear that her breathing wasn't as labored as it had been for the past few hours the evening before.

My sister took the first shift. She sat silently holding my mom's hand and filling her with positive energy. She spoke to my mom and just sat still with her. Earlier the day before—knowing death was near—my sister had placed the purple sheets on my mom's bed because they were the color of the crown chakra. The violet energy connects us to our spiritual self, purifying our thoughts and feelings, and bringing guidance, inner strength and wisdom. This night, my sister was my mom's spiritual guide.

At midnight I took over. It was officially Christmas Eve. My favorite day of the year. During my shift, I turned on an internet radio station and played my mom Christmas carols through my phone. I set the phone down on her pillow, next to her ear, and ran my hands through her hair singing *Silent Night* and *God Rest Ye Merry Gentlemen*. When my mom was still lucid, I put in a request that she make her exit on Christmas Eve. I felt a holy connection to that day and felt that my mom leaving on that day would represent something truly spiritual. She did not disappoint.

I talked. And played music. And told her I held more love in my heart for her than I did for any other person who ever lived. I thanked her for being the best mother a child could ever ask for. I told her I would see her again one day and that I would call upon her often after she was gone. I found three of her favorite songs online: Bette Midler's *The Wind Beneath My Wings*, Lawrence Welk's *The Anniversary Song* (a song played at my parents' wedding), and *The Battle Hymn Of The Republic*. It had always been one of her favorites. She used to sing it to me as a lullaby when I was a baby. It was only fitting that I played it for her lullaby as she drifted off to her final sleep.

My brother was at the helm for the third and final shift. It was almost 2 a.m. and it was clear that my mom was in the process of making her transition. Knowing it would be happening at any moment, I tapped my dad on the shoulder and told him to wake up. "It's happening," I said, as he struggled to remove the eye shades from his face. I hated to be the one to tell my dad that the love of his life was about to leave him. I wish I could have let him sleep through it all, but we all needed to be present for my mom at this time. I ran through the kitchen and down the hall to the bedroom where my sister had gone to sleep after her shift had ended a few hours earlier. Coincidentally, or ironically, or as the result of my mom's spiritual influence, my sister had set her alarm for 2 a.m.

Her alarm went off the minute I stepped into her room. As she reached over to the nightstand to turn it off, I peeked my head into the room and said, "It's time. Hurry." She bolted out of bed and the two of us quickly made our way back down the hallway and into the family room where my brother and dad were keeping watch over my mom.

My sister and I took our places at her bedside. My brother was holding her right hand, my father, on the opposite side of the bed, was holding her left. I sat at the foot of the bed and had my hand on her leg. My sister sat across from me, also with her hands on my mom.

We all watched as the blankets over my mom would rise and fall with each fading breath. One breath. Two breaths. Three breaths. Four breaths. My mom's breathing was slowing to about one breath every fifteen seconds. Five breaths, and . . . another breath never followed. She was gone. My brother called the time of death. 2:06 a.m. My mom's hands that had been cold for days, were suddenly filled with warmth. It was as if her spirit just left her body and exited out her fingertips. Floating like a feather being licked by the wind around the room, enveloping those who loved her so much. Her spirit. My mom's spirit. God, my mom was so spirited. I couldn't believe that her soul—her essence— would be doing anything less than dancing around the room, comforting us, wrapping us up in its beauty, giving us one final hug before retreating to the skies. Soaring into heaven. Perhaps led by the gentleman who had appeared at the foot of her bed a few days earlier. To be there with my mother at this sacred time of her life, was the greatest gift I have ever received. We—her family—were her ushers. Taking her hand and escorting her from this world to the next. Her children. Her husband. Handing her off to her angel guides as her final breath left her body. It was truly a religious experience. I couldn't help but wonder if my first breath was as soul-stirring to my mother as her last breath was to me.

My dad was slumped over my mom's body, sixty-four years of tears flowing from his eyes. My brother was holding her hand, saying the Lord's Prayer. My sister, full of her usual grace, wiped tears from her face and began doing what she did best: working out the next steps, the details. She called the hospice who called the funeral director and then she began cleaning up the family room. She started to wash bedding and towels, making it easier for the rest of us, because none of us could have done what my sister did that night.

My dad left my mom's side, retreated to the kitchen table, grabbed his journal and began to write:

Our "princess" passed away at 2:06 a.m. Saturday, December 24th.

I simply sat for a moment, assessed the situation, and looked at my mom one last time before the funeral home employees would come to take her away and make her look unrecognizable. I then went into my bedroom with Angie, closed the door and silently sobbed myself to sleep. I didn't run wailing into the street as I suspected I would. I didn't throw myself over my mom's body, unwilling to let go. I didn't refuse to release her hand or beg her to take another breath. No. I said my good-byes and went to bed. I thought that if I didn't make a big deal about it, that she really wouldn't be gone. That I'd come into the family room in the morning and there she would be, lying in bed, laughing, telling us to take some cookies home. The blanket would be moving. I just needed to walk away like it was any other day and I was simply saying goodnight and going into my room. I didn't want to be there when the funeral directors carted her out. I was afraid they would put her in a plastic bag and I'd have to see that. My mom didn't belong in a plastic bag. She belonged under a blanket, cared for like she was when she was alive. I didn't want her treated any differently in death. I have no idea what they did to her when they took her body out. I did not look.

I didn't see the men in the suits with the slicked-back hair carry my mom out the door. Perhaps Kitty Finazzo did. I didn't need to know that part of the story. I needed to sleep. And that's what I did. Knowing that tomorrow morning would be the first morning in forty-nine years, three months and twenty-four days that I'd wake up without a mother in my life.

After The Days

(On the first wedding anniversary after my mom's death)

MY DAD: I talked to your Mother today. I always talk to that pretty picture of her.

ME: What did you talk about?

MY DAD: I asked her if she knew what day it was.

ME: What did she say?

MY DAD: She said she didn't know.

ME: What did you say?

MY DAD: I told her it was our anniversary. She said she didn't know that. I told her it was sixty-five years! She said, "Oh yeah. Now I know. Now I know."

ME: In Heaven maybe they don't have calendars or celebrate holidays anymore.

MY DAD: I guess not. But I told her Happy Anniversary, anyway.

How does one go on without a mother in her life? I never thought I would be able to accomplish that feat.

My mom died Christmas Eve morning. Just as I had requested. The day that held so much spiritual energy for me, would now forever be the most sacred day of the year. We muddled through Christmas Eve and Christmas Day following my mom's death—spending the holiday with relatives, feeling strange that we were out and about, but also knowing that my mom wouldn't want us to be sitting at home mourning. Less than twenty-four hours after my mom had passed away, my dad, sister and I spent the evening driving down beautiful Lakeshore Drive in Grosse Pointe Shores looking at the Christmas light displays adorning the mansions. My mom loved doing this every year. We honored her by keeping the tradition alive. I felt her in the car with us that evening. And saw her spirit in every light that twinkled along the way.

The visitation took place the day after Christmas. Walking into the room at the funeral home where my mom was laid to rest was difficult. It was much easier a few days prior when Jack, the funeral director, gave us our tour. I had last seen my mom in her hospice bed just before the men with the slicked back hair came to take her away. Suddenly here she was, in her blue dress with the white sweater and the crystal buttons and the jewelry my sister and I picked out for her and the silver shoes I couldn't see. She didn't look at all like she looked that night. She didn't really look like my mother, in fact. Her hair was wrong, her coloring was off and the pink nails I had so lovingly painted had been painted over with a frosty shade of white. My mom's go-to color. Almost as if my mom somehow painted her own nails in the afterlife.

My mom's hands, crossed, rested upon her fancy blue dress. I laid my hand on top of hers and was startled by the coldness. All of her softness had disappeared. To the left of my mom's casket was a very large, beautiful floral display. I opened the small card accompanying the flowers and smiled as I read, "Millie, the greatest neighbor I could ever hope for. You were loved and will be missed. Kitty Finazzo." I closed the card, then walked over to the casket and said, "Mother, those flowers are from Kitty. Are you ready to take her off the shit list yet?" At that very moment, the first guest to walk through the door was Kitty Finazzo. I looked down at my mom with scolding eyes and said, "Be nice!" I greeted Kitty, hugged her, and walked her toward my mom's casket. I told her how much her friendship meant to my mom and dad. I could hear my mom scream "Bullshit!" from her astral plane. I looked up and smiled.

Mitch's eulogy was read that night by me at the funeral home, along with a beautiful eulogy by my brother, and another tribute by my cousin Bob, one of my mom's favorite humans. At the end of his piece, Bob pulled out a mini digital recorder and played a message from my mom she recorded a week earlier that said, "I'm Millie Goich, and I approve of this message." She had the crowd laughing, even after death.

Oh, and the sweatshirt was hung next to the casket thanking everyone for coming, just as she had wished.

The funeral took place the following day. It was freezing cold and sleeting. As Mitch Albom called it, "Perfect funeral weather." Hundreds of people paid their final respects to my mom that day, despite the slush and muck. At the cemetery, as we walked past her closed casket for the final time, Jack, the funeral director, encouraged us all to place our hands on the blue casket with the silver handles, leaving our finger-prints behind. Because no two fingerprints are alike, it would be our way of leaving a little bit of ourselves with my mom. I laid my palm flat on the casket, barely able to breathe. I then closed my fingers, drew my arm back, and fist bumped the casket one final time on the way out and said, "See ya later, Millie Goich."

The goodbyes came and went, I returned to my life in Los Angeles, I never made it to the Bob Seger concert—which took place the same day as my mom's funeral—and the world continued as normal. But my normal would never be the same again.

The hardest thing for me was not being able to call my mom on the phone. I never realized how many times a day I called my mom until my mom wasn't there to call any longer. If a problem would arise at home, I'd say, "I'm going to call my . . . oh wait . . . can't call her." I'd have a question about something in my life like, "How much did I weigh when I was born?" And suddenly I realized that the chief historian of our family was no longer there with answers. Anything we knew in our lives was all we would ever know. Her input was no longer.

I talk to my mom regularly. Occasionally I fall down on my knees in tears, asking her for assistance. Sometimes while driving home from work I'll turn off the radio and just have a conversation with my mom during my hour-long commute. I hear her talk back to me. And it's as if she never left.

I heeded my mom's advice, and never got the tattoo. However, I did get a bracelet, hand-etched that read, "Don't get a tattoo, you'll get hepatitis."

My dad adjusted as well as one would expect someone would after losing their partner of sixty-four years. He sold their house and moved to an independent living facility where he is surrounded by people, fed and taken care of. He works out three days a week and bowls on Fridays. My dad is a hot commodity at his new place of residence. The ratio of women to men in his facility is an astounding seven-to-one. The fact that he can walk without the aid of a walker, still holds a driver's license and has a good chunk of his hair still left, ensures that he will always have a bevy of beauties surrounding him at the breakfast and dinner table. That being said, he hasn't taken in a new friend yet and still remains loyal to my mom. An 8.5 x 11 photo of Millie in a red, white and blue party hat, sits on his dresser. He talks to the photo every morning when he rises and every evening before he goes to bed. He celebrates with the photo on holidays and anniversaries. Usually his conversations begin with, "I talked to your mother today . . ."

I talk to my dad now every day.

To my mom, "up there," I say, thank you for the inspiration to tell your story. And thank you for being the best mother a child could ever be placed in the hands of.

And thank you, especially, Mother, for helping me write this book.

Acknowledgements

Merriam-Webster defines a memoir as, "A narrative composed from personal experience. An account of something noteworthy." A more noteworthy event than the fourteen days documented here I have never experienced in my life. And I have so many people to thank for getting me through those days and to the point where you—the reader —hold this book in your hands.

Nothing I am could be possible without my mother's love, constant encouragement and undying belief in me. Mother, wherever you are "up there," thank you for guiding me through every word on these pages and for continuing to guide me through life. I love you beyond love and will see you again at our picnic in heaven.

Thank you father for working so hard for us your entire life and for stepping into mother's shoes after she left. You know what they say . . . "Abyssinia!"

Teddy Andreadis, my husband, my Mooley, my love, thank you for picking me so many years ago. To my sister Kristina, the yin to my yang, I couldn't have been blessed with a better friend. Without you I would have never made it through those fourteen days and beyond. To my brother Richard, thank you for loving me since I was a baby. Our "Goich Kids Act" was surely something spectacular and, if I weighed a little less, perhaps we could relive it again. Sara and Nicole, you are the children I never had. Always know that you're first and foremost in my heart. Darrell and Kathy, thank you for always treating our mother like your own. Auntie Dolores, you're far more than an aunt to me and I will never be able to thank you for the unending love you've given me. Cousins Karen, Jim, Bob (and extended Birach brood), you were siblings to me more than cousins. I love you all very much. To my BFF, Connie, only you know the extent to which our friendship has been stretched. You and I are in it for the long haul.

To Mitch Albom, thank you for being there for my mom during her final days, and for your constant belief in me. You don't have to do what you do, but you do—that's just how you roll. Thank you for providing her eulogy while she could still read it, which became the perfect start to this book. I am indebted. To Rosey, no one makes me laugh or has as much heart as you do. The entire Goich family loves you so much—especially your buddy Nick. To Cecilia and Michael, thank you for my mom's final blessings. To Laura, Tracy, Nancy, Carla and all of the helpers who loved and bathed and cared for my mom during those final days, I tip my heart to you.

Wendy Woodward Guarisco, this book wouldn't have been a book had it not been for your belief in it, and me. A thousand thank yous wouldn't be sufficient. Nena Madonia, by taking on this project, you made it a reality. I take a few of the thousand thank yous from Wendy's pile and hand them to you. Michael, Gavin, Hannah, Melanie, Ryan, Emily and everyone at Savio Republic/Post Hill, thank you for making this book a thing of beauty and for putting up with my constant "Well, shouldn't this be more like . . ." emails throughout this whole process. I know I'm a pain in the butt; my appreciation for bearing with me. To Jennie Freeburg, my early reader, second set of eyes and constant go-to in this process —the keys on my Macbook Air can't possibly type my sentiments and gratefulness.

To all of my high school and college friends, fellow Serbs (especially Kathie Anderson) and colleagues who visited in those final days and came out to my mom's funeral to support our family, your presence made our hearts a little less heavy. Love to all of my friends in cyberspace who encouraged me to start, continue and finish this memoir, despite every roadblock along the way. To Helen Landon, Dr. Monica Sarang and Jeffrey Johnson, thank you for keeping me together from head-to-toe.

To Steve Jobs for creating the laptop that created this entire book (even without the "H" key), and my Serta Perfect Sleeper upon which I was perched during much of this book's production, thank you.

And finally, to my four-legged children: Angie, Stella, Milly, JJ and the late Lulu, Oliver, Bowie, Zeke, Katy, Gabby, Buffy and Pom Pom who are at my mom's side right now. Life would be nothing without your unconditional love.

About the Author

Lisa Goich-Andreadis is an award-winning copywriter, major market talk radio host, blogger, journalist and former stand-up comedian. Graduating from Central Michigan University in 1984 with a Bachelor Of Applied Arts Degree in Journalism, she has spent her life dedicated to the written word, the spoken word and the arts. Lisa has worked for some of the biggest names and corporations in the literary and entertainment business such as Mitch Albom, Carole King, Robert Redford, ABC, The WB, CAA and Playboy. She has written ads for clients such as The American Red Cross, KFC, 7-Eleven, Thorn Apple Valley, and numerous TV and radio stations. As a talk radio host and producer, Lisa has worked for major market terrestrial radio stations such as KFI AM 640 in Los Angeles (America's #1 Talk Radio Station), the iconic WJR AM 760 in Detroit, KLSX / Los Angeles and KTLK / Los Angeles. Lisa currently serves as a senior project manager for the Jazz and Comedy genres of the prestigious GRAMMY Awards. Lisa's first book, *The Breakup Diary*, was published in 2002. She currently lives in Los Angeles with her husband, musician Teddy Andreadis (Guns 'n' Roses, Carole King, Alice Cooper, Billy Bob Thornton), and their four rescue dogs. She and her Maltese mix, Angie, work with hospice patients and their families, helping to make their transitions to the other side a loving, bonding and peaceful experience.